CACHE Level 2

Certificate in Understanding Behaviour that Challenges

Understanding Challenging Behaviour

Assessment 2

By

Dr Pedro Ramalho

and

Mr Sean Flynn

The Cache Level 2 Certificate in Understanding Behaviour that Challenges is fundamental and necessary part of the caring profession from carer to care home manager to mental healthcare professional, to progress their careers and better understand their clients.

Dr Pedro Ramalho wants you to know you can do this. It looks hard but it is not, it is easy, you only have to care. If you care for your client as you care for yourself, you will never be defeated in this profession, however little you think you know, for in truth if you care to such a level you are already one of the best carers in Britain today.
Which is why you are here, as a carer, for it is care that leads to the understanding of a patients challenging behaviour and from that understanding, that the behaviour can be improved, thus a patients quality of life is improved. When someone asks what you are   doing you can reply that you are literally improving someone's life. A noble goal with a noble end. Care and improvement of a patients life is the fundament of our profession. The eternal truth is that we are all humans…....being, and in trying just to be, all of us need care. That is why both you and I care, and your care is just as important, just as valid and just as necessary as my care. Let us care together!

Mr Flynn interprets Dr Ramalho's thoughts and wisdom to the best of his ability. In addition to being Dr Ramalho's legal magician, Mr Flynn agrees with Dr Ramalho's principles of care and the reaffirmation that we are all in a caring profession, no matter how humble our position our care matters and is important. It is our profession and we are all professionals. Which is why we wrote these books, to enable you to not only pass but dominate your profession, with care and hard work you too can achieve what Dr Ramalho has achieved, 800 out of 800 points from the Cache Level 2 Certificate in Understanding behaviour that Challenges . Yes it is possible, yes it is achievable, his work is in your hands and it is this very work that gained that perfect score. Do as he does and you will only get better and care more, about everybody, especially yourself! Enjoy!

CACHE Level 2

Certificate in Understanding Behaviour that Challenges

Assessment 2

Answer to question **1: Describe a range of communication methods**.

All behaviour is a form of communication, therefore all behaviour can be interpreted as a **form of expression**. Here we will lean how behaviour can be used as a form of expression and the range of communication methods available to support individuals especially those with communication difficulties or disorders.

Communicating

When dealing with communication difficulties and your strategies and care plan, you look to your basic building blocks of **'understanding challenging behaviour'**, **'the law'**, and **'policies and procedures'** of your company.

A person centred approach is required. You have to look to the individual uniquely in beginning your journey of effective and successful communication with an individual with a communication disorder. You will have to consider their **barriers to communication** and **how to overcome them** and the importance of **adapting communication needs to suit the individual**.

You will need to understand the importance of **positive reinforcement, avoiding confrontation, support for individuals with challenging behaviour, recording and reporting incidents of behaviour that challenges**.

Different Communication methods

How behaviour can be interpreted a form of expression.

It is important to understand the reasons for behaviour, especially if the behaviour is challenging, or in other words is '**a cause for concern with negative implications for themselves, their families and their carers.**'

Before you can manage difficult behaviour it is necessary to understand what the underlying causes are. For example, self-harming may be a response to a need for communication, feelings of pain or frustration. Since behaviour is a form of communication it is important to observe the behaviour if we want to understand its message. We need to try and establish 'what' it is that the individual is telling us. Is it that the individual needs something, or wants something, or does the behaviour communicate the **feelings** of the individual.

Behaviour that challenges may be be a way of communicating some common issues regarding the individual with challenging behaviour such as:

1. **Hunger**

2. **Pain**

3. **Boredom**

4. **Anxiety**

5. **Discomfort**

Challenging behaviour is the individual telling us that something is wrong, it is up to us to work out what that is, to help the individual. They cannot, so we have to.

Challenging behaviour may also be a way for the individual to cope with certain situations, such as anxiety regarding a new school or attending the dentist (Who enjoys that experience, challenging behaviour or no!). It could be that certain situations are **over challenging** the individual. It is important to recognise the **triggers** (what causes the individual to display challenging behaviour) and the **associated behaviours** (the behaviour displayed). If the challenging behaviour is a **coping mechanism** for the individual with challenging behaviour, **coping strategies** within your care plan can be put in place to help the challenged individual.

Forms of communications

When dealing with the individual with challenging behaviour it is important to find **the most effective ways to communicate. The more effective the communication,** the **more effective your care**.

Common forms of communication:

1. **Written messages**

2. **Gestures**

3. **Body language**

4. **Facial expressions**

5. **Use of pictures**

6. **Symbols**

7. **Signing**

Coping through routine

It is common for individuals with autism to show signs of obsession or ritualistic behaviour, this is because such obsessions and rituals help the individual to cope, especially if they begin to feel **over challenged**. Such **obsessive behaviour** and **learned responses** can be a way for the individual to cope with everyday challenges. Challenges we would take for granted.

The inner child

Individuals with challenging behaviour tend to react like children to their environment, for in a sense they are, just like a child is not fully responsible for their actions due to their young age so are individuals with challenging behaviour, due to the sheer fact they have a problem they cannot deal with alone. They need help, and often they lack the capacity to help themselves, so like parents we are there to care for them, and like children if you take away an object an individual with challenging behaviour is obsessed with you are likely to have them demonstrate challenging behaviour.

Routine helps children to understand their environment and makes the environment **reliable** and **predictable** which it makes the environment feel safer. If you feel 'at home' somewhere you are very comfortable with your environment. Like children individuals with challenging behaviour like the same. **A safe, reliable and predictable world.**

Like all of us, individuals with challenging behaviour will accumulate habits over time in such an environment. Especially when you consider some individuals with challenging behaviour will spend the vast majority of their time in this safe and predictable environment.

The son may visit the father in the care home for a short time, but the father lives there and will have his own habits. The individual with challenging behaviour may want the same seat everyday, the same programs on the TV at set times or a set bedtime etc.

Different forms of communication that can be used

Communication is about sending a message and for communication to be effective both parties must understand the message. Some individuals with challenging behaviour have great difficulties in communicating effectively. Some may have difficulties with their speech (slurring from a stroke, or Echolalia from autism), have very limited speech (a limited lexicon due to deep psychological issues) or cannot speak at all ("That deaf, dumb and blind kid can sure play a mean pinball!").

Communication can become very challenging and in some cases impossible if you just stick with talking so other ways of communicating will have to be used.

Other forms of communications

1. Signing
2. Symbols
3. Gestures
4. Written communications
5. Voice Output Communication Aids (VOCA)

Augmentative and Alternative Communication (AAC)

Augmentative and Alternative Communication is a term to define what kinds of additional help some individuals with challenging behaviour need. It is used to describe the different ways of communicating, either to **support** speaking (augmentative) or **instead** of speaking (alternative).

There are two main types of AAC (Augmentative and Alternative Communication) systems.

1   **Unaided communications**

Unaided communications are methods that don't use additional equipment. The methods are as the name suggest unaided, without aid. The methods use what nature has provided, your hands, body and face to provide body language, facial expressions, pointing and signing.

2   **Aided communications**

Aided communications are any communication methods **that needs additional aids** other than yourself, that you cannot do just with your body, hands and face. Aided communications can be '**low-tech**' (signs and cards) to '**high-tech**' (Electronic devices to aid communication like Voice Output Communication Aids VOCA).

High-tech aids usually need batteries or electricity to work and cover a variety of AAC systems (Augmentative and Alternative Communication). These AAC systems make use of whatever physical movement the user can control, which could be their hands, feet, head or eyes. Such as the AAC system that Dr Stephen Hawking famously used. High tech systems allow the individual choices and creates messages using pictures, symbols, words or letters that can be linked to an electronic voice. It's thanks to Dr Hawking's AAC system that I learned about a doughnut shaped universe so way to go!

Low-tech aids are aids that **don't need batteries** to work, such as picture or symbol books or boards.

Use of symbols for communication support

Symbols are an excellent way of communicating a lot of information quickly. Which is why there are import things such as **road signs** and **danger signs** (exits, hazards etc.) and because of this signs are everywhere, food labels, mobile phone operation, speed warnings. As we use symbols to communicate quickly and efficiently certain proscribed things, so symbols can be used by individuals with challenging behaviour to quickly and efficiently communicate, especially if they find speech difficult.

Symbols that help individuals with challenging behaviour communicate can be:

1   Arranged on communication boards.

2   Displayed on a computer screen.

3   Found in communication books.

The individuals with challenging behaviour can choose a symbol that will indicate what they want to communicate. Sometimes a symbol has the word or words written underneath it, which helps if the **'listener'** in the conversation is not familiar with the symbols presented to them.

Symbol Systems

There are many different symbol systems in use around the UK, but they all aim to **support** an individual with challenging behaviour's communication using a **picture format**. As each symbol system has different features, it is important to choose the right one for the user.

(Workbook 2 CACHE Level 2 Certificate in Understanding Behaviour that Challenges Section 1 Page 7.)

1   Picture of a glass/drink

This symbol can be used to communicate that the individual with challenging behaviour is thirsty.

2   Picture of a knife and fork

This symbol can be used to communicate that the individual with challenging behaviour is hungry.

3   Picture of a lounge chair

This symbol can be used to communicate that the individual with challenging behaviour wants their evening break.

4   Picture of a bed

This symbol can be used to communicate that the individual with challenging behaviour is ready for bedtime.

5   Picture of a bus

This symbol can be used to communicate that the individual with challenging behaviour is ready to travel.

6   Picture of shopping bags

This symbol can be used to communicate that the individual with challenging behaviour wishes to shop.

Minimal Speech Approach

The '**Minimal Speech Approach**' is one of several strategies that can be implemented into your behaviour and support plan and your care plan in general. 'Minimal Speech Approach' is a way of communicating to adults and children with '**severe communication delay**' as there is solid evidence **that simplifying language helps the individual understand better**, and this in turn has a positive effect on the individual with challenging behaviour, **since it encourages communication**. With more interaction and responses.

The Minimal Speech Approach focuses on using just one or two keywords instead of a sentence. A strangely natural idea because it is what we do all the time when visiting a foreign country. We learn very simple base words to communicate in a loud voice. For example it would be very challenging for the individual with challenging behaviour to understand "If you get your coat and shoes on we can go to the park now!" instead you can focus on handing the individual their coat and say 'coat' and 'shoes'.

When using the Minimal Speech Approach it is advisable to focus on nouns (**simple objects**, dog, bag, coat) and verbs (**simple doing things**, walk, run, swim, sit) rather than complex words that need context, like adjectives (big, heavy, fast), prepositions (at, in, behind), pronouns (she, he, mine), or time concepts (yesterday, tomorrow, this morning).

Signing

Signing is when individuals use their hands to make different movements or shapes to communicate. Although deaf people have a number of complex sign languages, we generally have a number of basic signs that we use in day to day life which became the inspiration for more complex sign languages and signing in general. We stick our thumbs up to indicate everything is ok, we wave vigorously from a distance to say hello and indicate our presence, and during the second world war we would put up two fingers to show faith in British victory.

Signing can help individuals understand what is being said to them. Signing can be used with or without speech. **For signing to be effective both communication parties must understand what the sign means**. There are many different signing systems used in the UK, one of the most common is the '**British Sign Language**' sign system.

Examples of signs used in British Sign Language.

(**Workbook 2 p9**)

1   Left hand waving

Hello.

2 Left hand waving after conversation

Goodbye.

3 Left hand with raised thumb twisted to the left

Good morning.

4 Left hand with top two fingers outstretched twisted down clockwise

Good afternoon

5 Both hands thumb hidden twisting down

Good night

6 Left hand thumb hidden twisting down anti clockwise

Thanks/please

Body Language and facial expressions

In conversation we naturally add meaning to what we are saying by using facial expressions such as:

1 Smiling

2 Frowning

3	Raising your eyebrows

4	Winking

5	Shaking or nodding their head

6	Gestures like waving goodbye

For individuals with challenging behaviour with limited speech or no speech, facial expressions and gestures are very important ways to help with communication. However as simple and natural as facial expressions are, there are some individuals with challenging behaviour with such physical impairments that even facial expressions and gestures are difficult. For example, 'no' could be just looking down instead of the individual with challenging behaviour vigorously nodding their head, whilst looking up can be 'yes'.

For some individuals with challenging behaviour their main communication is expressed through their challenging behaviour, rather than verbalising communication, for example an adult hitting their head when distressed or in pain, or a child starting to pinch themselves when they become bored.

When attempting to communicate with an individual with challenging behaviour who has communication issues, **it is important to take the time to find out what the individual's preferred method of communication is** and also **consistent with the method they use**.

Written messages

Written messages are another natural alternative to verbal communication. Although it can take more time to communicate in writing, more complex information can be imparted. Providing the individuals with challenging behaviour can understand enough to read and write you can use a **chart** or **keyboard** to help the individual with challenging behaviour to help them communicate. The individual with challenging behaviour can **spell out messages for others** to read using **pen and paper**, a **laptop**, **keyboard** or **mobile phone**.

Voice Output Communication Aids (VOCAs)

VOCAs include a wide range of devices that are designed to help individuals who are unable to speak or have severe vocal communication issues. A VOCA produces spoken words to help the individual with challenging behaviour to communicate.

Some VOCAs store words or phrases which allow the user to put messages together which are then spoken out by the device. There are many types of VOCAs available so it is important to seek **independent professional advice** to ensure that the individual with challenging behaviour
gets **the right device to meet their needs.**

Makaton

Makaton is a language programme that helps individuals with challenging behaviour to communicate. It is designed to support spoken language using signs, symbols and speech which help provide extra clues about what someone is saying. Using signs can help individuals who have no speech or whose speech is unclear. Using symbols can help people who have limited speech or who cannot or prefer not to sign.

Makaton can be used to:

1   Share thoughts, choices and emotions.

2   Label real objects, pictures, photos and places.

3   Take part in games.

4   Listen to, read and tell stories.

5   Create recipes, menus and shopping lists.

6   Write letters and messages.

7   Help people find their way around public buildings.

Makaton is a language programme designed to provide a means of communication to individuals who cannot communicate efficiently by speaking. **The Makaton language programme** has been used with individuals who have **cognitive impairments**, **autism**, **Down syndrome**, specific language impairment, multisensory impairment and acquired **neurological disorders** that have negatively affected the ability to communicate, including stroke patients.

The name "Makaton" is derived from the first letters of the names of three speech and language therapists who helped devise the programme in the 1970s, researchers Margaret Walker, and Katharine Johnston and Tony Cornforth (MaKaTon), colleagues from the Royal Association for Deaf people. Makaton is a registered trade mark of The Makaton Charity, which was established in 2007.

Signalong

Signalong is an 'augmentative' communication system based on signs adapted from **British Sign language**. It helps with whatever language can be spoken or understood and is used together with speech, not instead of it.

Signalong is an alternative and augmentative key-word signing communication method used by those individuals with a speech, language and communication need. The Signalong methodology has been effectively used with individuals who have cognitive impairments, autism, Down's Syndrome, specific language impairment, multisensory impairment and acquired neurological disorders that have negatively affected the ability to communicate, including stroke patients and English as an additional language.

The name "Signalong" is derived from the understanding that wherever possible the sign is accompanied with speech, hence you "sign along with speech". The programme was devised in 1991 by Gill Kennard, a language teacher, Linda Hall, a science teacher who produced the illustrations and Thelma Grove, a speech and language therapist from the Royal College of Speech & Language Therapists.

Signalong is a registered trade mark of The Signalong Group, a charity established in 1994.

British Sign Language

British Sign Language (BSL) is a sign language used in the United Kingdom (UK), and is the first or preferred language of some deaf people in the UK; there are 125,000 deaf adults in the UK who use BSL plus an estimated 20,000 children. In 2011, 15,000 people, living in England and Wales, reported themselves using BSL as their main language. The language makes use of space and involves movement of the hands, body, face and head. Many thousands of people who are not deaf also use BSL, as hearing relatives of deaf people, sign language interpreters or as a result of other contact with the British deaf community.

Supporting Individuals to Communicate

Here are some basic principles to use to help individuals with challenging behaviour to communicate:

1   **Use the individuals name** at the start of a conversation so they know you are talking to   them.

2   **Use any special interest** individuals have to engage them and motivate them to take part in your conversation.

3   **Make sure individuals are paying attention** before speaking to them.

4   **Provide time** for individuals to respond as it may take longer for them to answer.

5   **Use visual supports** like symbols and pictures to help individuals with challenging behaviour understand and process what is conveyed to them more easily.

6   **Speak clearly and use short sentences**. Too much information can confuse and over   challenge.

7   When possible, **avoid questions such as 'why', 'where' and 'when'** as they can be difficult   for individuals with challenging behaviour to cope with.

Importance of communications

Being able to communicate effectively is one of the cornerstones of good care and a good care-plan, it is one of the most important skills an individual has in their lives. Almost everything we do in life requires communication of some sort.

For example:

1   Everyday tasks such as ordering food.

2   Buying goods and services.

3   Getting the care we need.

4   Getting from place to place.

5   Learning skills and knowledge.

6   Sorting out problems.

7   Making friends.

8   Having fun.

Answer to question 2: Describe the importance of non-verbal communication.

Some individuals with challenging behaviour have limited verbal communication skills and may not be able to communicate effectively to communicate their needs. Because of this individuals with challenging behaviour need alternative communication methods which are **non-verbal** such as gestures, sign language and symbols in order to communicate their thoughts, feelings, desires and needs. It is important that individuals with challenging behaviour have an alternative method of communicating if they cannot do so effectively verbally.

Importance of communicating

1   Allows individuals with challenging behaviour to **express feelings**.

2   Allows individuals with challenging behaviour to **ask questions**.

3   Allows individuals with challenging behaviour to **communicate what they need**.

4   Helps individuals with challenging behaviour to **develop relationships**.

5   Allows individuals with challenging behaviour to **feel better about themselves**.

6	Helps individuals with challenging behaviour to **gain some independence**.

7	Enables individuals with challenging behaviour to **be involved in decisions**.

8	Helps individuals with challenging behaviour to **gain employment**.

9	Enables individuals with challenging behaviour to **participate in education**.

Processing verbal information

When individuals with challenging behaviour struggle to make sense of verbal information they can be diagnosed with an **auditory processing disorder (APD)**. An **APD** is different from a hearing problem as an individual with challenging behaviour with APD is not deaf or hard of hearing, it is not the volume of sound that the individual with challenging behaviour has a problem with but the **interpretation of the sound**. In the same way we can hear French fine but do not understand the sounds of French. The difficulties for an individual with challenging behaviour is **auditory processing**.

Difficulties with auditory processing do not affect what is heard by the ear, but rather how the information is interpreted, or processed by the brain. Difficulties can occur when the individual with challenging behaviour tries to **process a sound**, either to hear and understand the sound or **'signal'**, **or when trying to form a response**.

An auditory processing disorder (APD) can interfere with speech and language. It can affect all areas of learning, especially reading and

spelling. As a lot of learning in schools and colleges relies on individuals being able to process verbal information.
Individuals with challenging behaviour who struggle to process information can have serious problems understanding lessons and therefore progressing. This has a detrimental effect throughout their lives, including but not limited to their chances of employment and education.

Individuals with challenging behaviour may have problems with:

Auditory Discrimination

The ability to recognise differences in sounds, such as the ability to identify words and sounds that are similar but whose meaning are different. Fish, dish, wish etc.

Auditory Memory

The ability to store and recall information which is given verbally. The individual with challenging behaviour may not be able to follow instructions given verbally or may struggle to recall information given verbally.

Auditory sequencing

The ability to remember or reconstruct the order of items in a list or the order of sounds in a word or syllable, meaning the individual may struggle to spell words as the letters would be in the wrong order. Very similar to dyslexia.

Auditory blending

The process of putting together sounds to form words.

Phonological awareness

The understanding that language is made up of individual sounds which are put together to form the words we write and speak, meaning the individual may have difficulty reading, writing and understanding spoken words.

Individuals with challenging behaviour may experience the following difficulties in communication:

1   **Speech sound disorders**

Difficulties in pronouncing sounds.

2   **Language disorders**

Difficulty in understanding what they hear and difficulty in expressing themselves using words.

3   **Cognitive-communication disorders**

Difficulty with perception, memory, awareness, reasoning, judgement, intellect and imagination.

4   **Stuttering disorders**

Interruption of the flow of speech including hesitation, repetition or prolongation of sounds and words.

5   **Voice disorders**

Where volume is too loud or too soft.

Although non-verbal communication is important to help individuals with challenging behaviour who have such disorders to communicate. It is also very important to know about the above disorders for without such knowledge it would be very easy to misdiagnose an individual with challenging behaviour. Maybe instead of dyslexia they have a language disorder, has the individual a deep psychological problem or do they in fact have a cognitive-communication disorder, it will be your job to find out.

Auditory processing disorder

Auditory processing disorder (**APD**), also known as **central auditory processing disorder** (**CAPD**), is an umbrella term for a variety of disorders that affect the way the brain processes auditory information. Individuals with APD usually have normal structure and function of the outer, middle and inner ear (**peripheral hearing**). However, they cannot process the information they hear in the same way as others do, which leads to difficulties in recognizing and interpreting sounds, especially the sounds composing speech. It is thought that these difficulties arise from **dysfunction in the central nervous system**.

Speech sound disorders

A **speech sound disorder (SSD)** is a speech disorder in which some speech sounds (**called phonemes**) in a child's (or, sometimes, an adult's) language are either not produced, not produced correctly, or are not used correctly. The term **protracted phonological development** is sometimes preferred when describing children's speech to emphasize the continuing development while acknowledging the delay.

Speech sound disorders may be subdivided into two primary types, **articulation disorders** (also called **phonetic disorders**) and **phonemic disorders** (also called **phonological disorders**). However, some may have a mixed disorder in which both articulation and phonological problems exist. Though speech sound disorders are associated with childhood, some *residual* errors may persist into adulthood.

Mixed speech sound disorders

In some cases phonetic and phonemic errors may coexist in the same person. In such case the primary focus is usually on the phonological component but articulation therapy may be needed as part of the process, since teaching a child how to use a sound is not practical if the child does not know how to produce it.

Residual errors

Even though most speech sound disorders can be successfully treated in childhood, and a few may even outgrow them on their own, errors may sometimes persist into adulthood rather than only being not age appropriate. Such persisting errors are referred to as "residual errors" and may remain for life.

Language disorders

Language disorders or language impairments are disorders that involve the processing of linguistic information. Problems that may be experienced can involve grammer (syntax and/or morphology), semantics (meaning), or other aspects of language. These problems may be receptive (involving impaired language comprehension), expressive (involving language production), or a combination of both. Examples include specific language impairment and aphasia, among others. Language disorders can affect both spoken and written language, and can also affect sign language; typically, all forms of language will be impaired.

Receptive language disorders

Receptive language disorders can be acquired or developmental (most often the latter). When developmental, difficulties in spoken language tend to occur before three years of age. Usually such disorders are accompanied by expressive language disorders.

However, unique symptoms and signs of a receptive language disorder include: struggling to understand meanings of words and sentences, struggling to put words in proper order, and inability to follow verbal instruction. Treatment options include: language therapy, special education classes for children at school, and a psychologist if accompanying behavioural problems are present.

Expressive language disorders

Unlike those with a speech disorder, the problem with expressive language disorders pertains not only to the voice and articulation, but to the mental formation of language itself.

Expressive language disorders can occur during a child's development or they can be acquired. This acquisition usually follows a normal neurological development and is brought about by a number of causes such as head trauma or irradiation.

Features of an expressive language disorder vary, but have certain features in common such as: limited vocabulary, inability to produce complex grammar, and more lexical errors.

Experts that commonly treat such disorders include speech pathologists and audiologists.

Cognitive-communication disorders

Neurocognitive disorders (NCDs), also known as cognitive disorders, are a category of mental health disorders that primarily affect cognitive abilities including learning, memory, perception, and problem solving. Neurocognitive disorders include delirium and **mild and major neurocognitive disorder** (previously known as **dementia**). They are defined by deficits in cognitive ability that are acquired (as opposed to developmental), they typically represent decline, and may have an underlying brain pathology. The DSM-5 defines six key domains of cognitive function: executive function, learning and memory, perceptual-motor function, language, complex attention, and social cognition.

Stuttering disorders

Stuttering, also known as stammering, is a speech disorder in which the flow of speech is disrupted by involuntary repetitions and prolongations of sounds, syllables, words or phrases as well as involuntary silent pauses or blocks in which the person who stutters is unable to produce sounds. The term *stuttering* is most commonly associated with involuntary sound repetition, but it also encompasses the abnormal hesitation or pausing before speech, referred to by people who stutter as *blocks*, and the prolongation of certain sounds, usually vowels or semivowels. According to Watkins et al., stuttering is a disorder of "**selection, initiation, and execution of motor sequences necessary for fluent speech production**." For many people who stutter, repetition is the primary problem. The term "stuttering" covers a wide range of severity, encompassing barely perceptible impediments that are largely cosmetic to severe symptoms that effectively prevent oral communication. In the world, approximately four times as many men as women stutter, encompassing 70 million people worldwide, or about 1% of the world's population.

Feelings and attitudes

Stuttering could have a significant negative cognitive and affective impact on the person who stutters. It has been described in terms of the analogy to an iceberg, with the immediately visible and audible symptoms of stuttering above the waterline and a broader set of symptoms such as negative emotions hidden below the surface. Feelings of embarrassment, shame, frustration, fear, anger, and guilt are frequent in people who stutter, and may actually increase tension and effort, leading to increased stuttering. With time, continued exposure to difficult speaking experiences may crystallize into a negative self-concept and self-image. Many perceive stutterers as less intelligent due to their dis-fluency; however, as a group, individuals who stutter tend to be of above average intelligence. A person who stutters may project his or her attitudes onto others, believing that they think he or she is nervous or stupid. Such negative feelings and attitudes may need to be a major focus of a treatment program. Many people who stutter report a high emotional cost, including jobs or promotions not received, as well as relationships broken or not pursued.

Acquired stuttering

In rare cases, stuttering may be acquired in adulthood as the result of a neurological event such as a head injury, tumour, stroke, or drug use. The stuttering has different characteristics from its developmental equivalent: it tends to be limited to part-word or sound repetitions, and is associated with a relative lack of anxiety and secondary stuttering behaviours. Techniques such as **altered auditory feedback**, which may promote decreasing dis-fluency in people who stutter with the developmental condition, are not effective with the acquired type.

Psychogenic stuttering may also arise after a traumatic experience such as a grief, the breakup of a relationship or as the psychological reaction to physical trauma. Its symptoms tend to be homogeneous: the stuttering is of sudden onset, and associated with a significant event. It is constant and

uninfluenced by different speaking situations, and there is little awareness or concern shown by the speaker.

Voice disorders

Voice disorders: are medical conditions involving abnormal pitch, loudness or quality of the sound produced by the larynx and thereby affecting **speech** production. These include:

- Puberphonia
- Chorditis
- Vocal fold nodules
- Vocal fold cysts
- Vocal cord paresis
- Reinke's edema
- Spasmodic dysphonia
- Foreign accent syndrome
- Bogart–Bacall syndrome
- Laryngeal papillomatosis
- Laryngitis

Answer to question 3: Describe the barriers to communication.

Individuals with challenging behaviour may display behaviour that challenges because they are unable to communicate well enough to have their needs met, and this can lead naturally enough to frustration, anxiety, fear and distress.

The Importance of needs

Maslow's hierarchy of needs concludes that individuals with challenging behaviour must have basic needs fulfilled such as food, heat, water and rest before being able to focus on higher needs such as learning or relationships. In most cases regardless of the need, if the need is not being met there is likely to be a display of challenging behaviour. Therefore meeting the needs of the individual with challenging behaviour is a priority to continue good care.

Barriers to communication

Barriers to communication are also barriers to good care and so the barriers should be breached.

Example 1: Siobhan

Siobhan can't explain verbally that she is hungry. She starts to scream and cry and when she sees other residents with food she becomes aggressive, trying to take food from them.

Siobhan's communication barrier is that she cannot communicate effectively using verbal communication. This barrier leads to her being unable to effectively say she is hungry, or indeed what she wants to eat. Frustration at a lack of ability to communicate ones basic need to be fed on top of being reduced to accept what is given regardless of quality naturally materialises. In Siobhan's case it manifests itself in the challenging behaviour of screaming, crying and eventual violence.

Understanding the communication barriers allows you as in Siobhan's case to put in place strategies within your care-plan to support Siobhan and allow her to communicate effectively and thus help her fulfil her need of food and desire for something yummy. For example a sign to indicate when she is hungry and a more complex communication system like writing, British Sign Language, or Makaton to effectively communicate her specific desires.

Types of Barriers to communications

1	Individuals with challenging behaviour can have **learning disabilities** which can lead to problems interpreting information verbally.

 2	The individual with challenging behaviour may be **unable to access written information**.

3	Individuals with challenging behaviour can have **difficulties with speech**.

4	Individuals with challenging behaviour may have **cognitive impairment** and may struggle to understand technical language and jargon.

5	Individuals with challenging behaviour may have **a lack of concentration** and **short attention spans**.

6	Some individuals with challenging behaviour may **need support in understanding the spoken word**.

7   Some Individuals with challenging behaviour may **have a fear of communicating socially** especially if they have been laughed at, teased or bullied in the past and have lost trust in others.

8   Some individuals with challenging behaviour may **have a hearing impairment** which can cause communication difficulties.

Answer to question 4: Describe ways to overcome barriers to communication.

Types of Barriers to communications and ways to overcome them.

1   Individuals with challenging behaviour **can have learning disabilities** which can lead to problems interpreting information verbally.

Speak more slowly than you normally would to give them time to process the information and understand what you are saying.

2   The individual with challenging behaviour may be **unable to access written information**.

Provide information in an alternative format such as 'easy read'. Information can be made easier
To understand by breaking it down in to shorter sentences or using images and symbols to help explain what the text is about. It is advisable to use bigger text (a minimum of 16 point font) and use bullet points rather than large pieces of written text.

3   Individuals with challenging behaviour **can have difficulties with speech**. Provide speech and language therapy.

4   Individuals with challenging behaviour may have **cognitive impairment** may struggle to understand technical language and jargon.

Avoid technical vocabulary and jargon. Use simple words and fewer syllables where possible.

5   Individuals with challenging behaviour may have a **lack of concentration** and **short attention spans**.

Choose a quiet place to talk, with no distractions. Keep conversations short and to the point.

6   Some individuals with challenging behaviour may **need support in understanding the spoken word**.

Use systems like Signalong or Makaton to support them in understanding spoken information.

7   Some Individuals with challenging behaviour may have **a fear of communicating socially** especially if they have been laughed at, teased or bullied in the past and have lost trust in others.

Provide such individuals with social situations in a safe environment with people who will show understanding and empathy and give them the time needed to process information and be able to engage in conversation.

8   Some individuals with challenging behaviour may have **a hearing impairment** which can cause communication difficulties.

Use signing and think about the environment provided – reduce background noise for example.

Receptive language

Another method of overcoming barriers to communication is receptive language. Receptive language means understanding the words and sentences used and is the foundation for all communication and language skills. To support receptive language skills and thus support the individual with challenging behaviour understand you can:

1   Get the attention of the he individual with challenging behaviour you are speaking to, before asking a question.

2   Begin an instruction using the individuals name.

3   Keep instructions or information short.

4   Avoid the use of complex verbal instructions or information. Keep is short and simple.

5   Use positive instructions and minimise the use of negative instructions such as 'stop' or 'don't'. Be exact and specific let the individual with challenging behaviour know exactly what you want them to do.

6   Provide 'waiting' time. Be patient and wait for a response and don't immediately repeat the instruction or question. **Do not overchallange the individual with challenging behaviour**.

Answer to question 5: Explain how communication can be adapted to meet the needs and preferences of each individual.

Communication is the giving and receiving of information, in other words the imparting and/or exchanging of information by speaking, writing, or using some other medium, and because it is the foundation of what we do in everyday life it is important to find appropriate ways of communicating with individuals with challenging behaviour.

When communicating with individuals with challenging behaviour such as autism or dementia for example it is essential to think carefully about the individuals with challenging behaviour and their needs and preferences. As per the current principles of care and its panoply and accoutrements everything is now **a person centred approach** rather than a catch all institutionalized approach. So the individual is important.

Everybody is different, and will think and communicate differently.

Everybody communicates a lot everyday. We give many messages to the people we communicate with, not just in what we say (**The complexity of the communication**), but how we say it (**the tone and volume of the communication**), what body language we use (**what we are doing while we are communicating for example emphasizing salient points with hand gestures**).

Many individuals with challenging behaviour communicate because of needs and wants, others may want to share information or ask questions to better understand situations.

Choice of communication

When choosing and 'adapting communication' we need to observe the individual with challenging behaviour's reactions and learn what is their normal or accustomed behaviour. What type of communication works best, or what communication once adapted works most effectively. It is important when assessing the most effective communication method to think about how the individuals with challenging behaviour is feeling when communicating with them, are they comfortable, happy, sad, angry, frustrated, etc.

If the individual with challenging behaviour feels stressed or appears uncomfortable with eye contact it may be better to implement a strategy within your care-plan to adapt your communication with the individual with challenging behaviour, by sitting to the side of them away from their eyeline to reduce stress so the individual with challenging behaviour does not need to make so much eye contact.

Appropriate communication skills

By using appropriate communication skills you can provide better support to the individual with challenging behaviour, allowing them more freedom, independence and more positive life choices, this in turn makes the individual with challenging behaviour feel respected, valued and in control. Also better communication reduces an individual with challenging behaviour's frustration, social isolation and all the other negative **impacts and effects** of a lack of effective communication.

Adapting communication styles

Very often when communicating with individuals with challenging behaviour, there will be a need to adapt our communication styles from the norm to meet the needs and desires of individuals with challenging behaviour. Aids can be used to help individuals with challenging behaviour enhance their communication experience. If there is a barrier to communication such as difficulty talking, an apparent lack of understanding or displays of challenging behaviour, it is obviously important to identify the barrier to their communication so the barrier can be breached and better understanding follow. From the **identity of the barrier to communication** you can work out how best to adapt your communication style to best overcome the barrier to communication.

For some individuals with challenging behaviour body language can be a useful tool in communicating when the individual with challenging behaviour cannot express themselves effectively using spoken words alone.

Common examples of challenging behaviour that could indicate a barrier to communication:

1	The individual with challenging behaviour moving back and forth

2	The individual with challenging behaviour moving away from the person talking to them.

3	The individual with challenging behaviour swearing.

4	The individual with challenging behaviour using repetitive phrases, out of context.

5	The individual with challenging behaviour stays silent.

These types of challenging behaviour highlight a communication problem of some kind and the frustration of the individual with challenging behaviour at not having their needs or desires met.

Golden rules when adapting communications

Here are some golden rules when you adapt any communications you have with individuals with challenging behaviour.

1	What is the purpose of the communication, what do you need to know, or what information do you need to give the individual?

2	How long do they need to process the information and give a response?

3	What is their ability to listen? You may need to keep conversations and instructions short.

4   Be intentional with body language. Make your body language obvious.

5   Be intentional with your language, use words the individuals with challenging behaviour can understand and connect with.

6   Make good eye contact, unless it makes the individual with challenging behaviour uncomfortable.

7   Allow the individual with challenging behaviour enough personal space, some individuals with challenging behaviour feel uncomfortable when too close to others.

8   Watch for responses and create an environment that the individual with challenging behaviour feels comfortable with.

9   Create a calm environment and don't insist on conversation. Let the communication flow at it's own speed.

10   Find visuals like illustrations, flash cards or photographs if individuals with challenging behaviour struggle with speech.

11   Slow speech down if necessary.

12   Use visual timetables or calendars to help explain difficult concepts like future dates and important appointments.

13   Keep background noise down.

It's not all talk

Although a lot of the communication we do with individuals with challenging behaviour are verbal, the majority of our communication or the information transferred is by our body language (55%) followed by the tone of our voice (38%). **The words of our communication make up only 7% of our communication.**

Answer to question 6: Describe the effects that your communication can have on others.

As individuals with challenging behaviour impact and effect themselves and others with their challenging behaviour, you also can cause impacts and effects with your communication on others. It is important to be aware of your own communication, both verbal and non-verbal. It is important to make sure your communication does not over challenge the individual with challenging behaviour and become a trigger for a display of challenging behaviour. Remember individuals with challenging behaviour need to be treated with **respect,** and a **professional** approach is not only essential at all times, it is also the **law**.

Communication styles that could cause displays of challenging behaviour from individuals with challenging behaviour.

1 **Raising your voice** unnecessarily or shouting angrily.

2 **Showing irritation** through the tone of your voice.

3 **Embarrassing the individual** with challenging behaviour especially in front of others as this can humiliate the individual with challenging behaviour.

4 Being **sarcastic.**

5   Using terms individuals with challenging behaviour **don't understand** or using puns and play on words.

6   Using **confrontational** body-language or being **threatening**.

7   Showing **anger** through facial expression.

8   Being **impatient**.

9   **Not responding** to the needs of the individual with challenging behaviour.

10   **Invading** the individual with challenging behaviour's personal space.

Negative Communication

These examples of negative communication styles or strategies contribute to **negative communication, to the detriment of the individual with challenging behaviour. Negative communication means bad care**. Lets look at an example of negative communication regarding Sarah an individual with challenging behaviour.

Sarah takes a long time to get ready for school in the mornings and her carer is impatient with her. The carer shows her frustration by sighing, rushing her and taking things off Sarah to do them for her to speed her up, rather than allowing her the time to do things for herself. Sarah doesn't like being rushed and becomes stressed and anxious. She starts to refuse to go to school because she finds getting ready too distressing.

With this example one wonders why the carer has bothered to enter the caring profession at all and you would forgive such dire care only from people who have no choice. Regardless Sarah's care has to be improved so let's get to it.

Sarah's function of behaviour is to avoid school, on speaking to Sarah the reason for the avoidance of school is that getting ready for school is too stressful. Further investigation reveals the above example in all it's ham fisted glory. Let us begin.

Sarah takes a long time to get ready for school in the mornings

The carer knows that Sarah takes a long time to get ready for school. The carer needs to first of all give Sarah more time. More time for Sarah and more time for the carer, so the carer does not feel impatient.

Her carer is impatient with her.

With more time there will be less need to be impatient.

The carer shows her frustration by sighing

Do not show frustration. It effects the individual with challenging behaviour negatively just in the same way most people do not want to encounter frustration when trying to master hard tasks. What is easy for the carer can be tremendously difficult for the individual with challenging behaviour. That's why you need patience because that's why patients are called patients. You are the carer they are your patients. So have some patience.

The carer should at the minimum say nothing. A professional carer should have the professionalism to not appear as the child in this scenario. The carer needs to get a grip and perform their important tasks quietly and professionally.

Rushing her

Do not 'rush' individuals with challenging behaviour. Nobody likes being rushed especially if an individual is so challenged they cannot rush even if they wanted too. This negative behaviour from the carer is guaranteed to bring forth a display of challenging behaviour from Sarah, and who could blame her, she has informed the carer very clearly that she needs a lot of time to get ready. So what does the carer do, rush! Obviously this carers motto is if a jobs worth doing, it's worth doing in a rush, good going. I'm beginning to feel pretty sorry for Sarah at this point.

Taking appropriate responsibilities off Sarah, for the carer to do themselves to speed Sarah up, rather than allowing her the time to do things for herself

So how does this carer think Sarah is going to learn things for herself? What things is the carer taking from Sarah and doing herself. The girl needs a lot of time to get ready and wants to do things herself. **Some basic independence**. Tasks that are designed to be best performed or understood alone. Brushing teeth, the loo, tying up ones own shoelaces, dressing one self. If Sarah is prevented from learning such things her chances at a free independent life is damaged.

Sarah doesn't like being rushed and becomes stressed and anxious. She starts to refuse to go to school because she finds getting ready too distressing.

Of course Sarah doesn't like being rushed and gets anxious with the carer. The solution to this daily nightmare is simply refuse to go school. So Sarah's carer must provide more time for Sarah to prepare for school, the carer should not show frustration, at all. The carer should not sigh, rush and by God should not take over tasks the individual with challenging behaviour is willing and able to do, albeit a bit slowly. More time and patience and a far better caring attitude will see a happier Sarah, a happier school and eventually a happier carer, Deus Vult!

Answer to question 7: Explain the importance of positive reinforcement.

It is best to stay positive and care in a positive manner, but why? Positive reinforcement is thought to be the most effective way of dealing with individuals with challenging behaviour. Positive reinforcement is a primary tool of support and supportive strategies. Positive reinforcement helps individuals with challenging behaviour learn new positive behaviour such as new ways of coping with challenging situations, managing their own behaviour or finding distractions when they find situations upsetting or difficult to deal with.

Positive reinforcement

When a desired behaviour is positively reinforced through reward or praise it is likely to be repeated. For best results the positive reinforcement should be given directly after a display of desired behaviour. This is to firmly and immediately tie the desired behaviour to the reward in the individual with challenging behaviour's mind.

Illustration of positive behaviours

Before:

Challenging behaviour

Behaviour desired is displayed:

Certain desired behaviour is performed

Immediately after desired behaviour:

Praise/reward offered as an incentive for the behaviour to be repeated.

Incentive to desired behaviour

When choosing a **reinforcer**, or **incentive** to desired behaviour it is important to as usual consider the individual and their needs and wants.

1. What has motivated them in the past?

2. What do they like or desire?

3. Make the reinforcer appropriate for the behaviour being targeted. Is the reinforcer to stop or avoid certain challenging behaviour, or is it to reinforce new or rarer desired positive behaviour.

Types of reinforcement

There are three general types of reinforcement:

1 **Positive**

The individual with challenging behaviour gets what they want.

2 **Negative**

The individuals with challenging behaviour is punished by having something they want removed.

3 **Intermittent**

Sometimes the individuals with challenging behaviour gets what they want but inconsistently.

Consistency

It is important that everyone involved in the care of individuals with challenging behaviour follow consistent approaches making positive reinforcement the natural choice for your reinforcement needs.

Examples of reinforcers

1 Having a drink with a friend.

2 Going to an event, such as a concert or sporting event.

3 Giving free time.

4 Verbal praise

5 Giving individuals with challenging behaviour tasks that they actually enjoy.

6 Giving a choice of outing

7   Tokens of achievement and merit like gold stars, or A+.

8   Awarding certificate or badges for meritorious behaviour.

Important factors of positive reinforcement

1   The reinforcer should not be something the individual with challenging behaviour has access to. It's not much of a reward to receive something you already have.

2   Accordingly do not give free access to the reward, as this will give the individual with challenging behaviour nothing to work towards. If a treasure is free and everywhere it is no treasure at all so why bother being motivated if you can have the reward for free.

3   Visual clues can work well, such as a chart with stars or ticks on, so the individual with challenging behaviour can see their progress. Remember Blue Peter, they sure got a lot of bottle tops from their large charts during charity drives.

4   The individual with challenging behaviour must feel that the goal set is achievable and that the reinforcement attainable.

5   Make requests for the desired behaviour very clear and concise so that the individual with challenging behaviour fully understands what is expected of them.

6   Always use verbal praise.

7   Fade reinforcers by offering less and less as the desired behaviour becomes the norm and eventually only give verbal praise to slowly teach the individual with challenging behaviour that the desired behaviour is the expected behaviour and no longer needs rewards.

8   A written contract may be useful to show all the details of the desired behaviour clearly, especially for individuals with challenging

behaviour who struggle with verbal communication. Symbols or pictures can be used to support the understanding of a contract as this may be considered a very abstract concept for some individuals with challenging behaviour.

9   Model the desired behaviour. Be the example for the individual with challenging behaviour to follow. After all if you cannot be asked to display the desired positive behaviour then why should the individual with challenging behaviour.

10   Always try to end the day as you started it on a positive note, even if it has been a bad day. A bad word at the end of the day can have the individual with challenging behaviour stressed until the next care meeting.

11   It is worth noting that rewards do not have to be continually material. One-to-one time with family and friends can be even more rewarding than a simple treat and better for a man's soul too.

Example of a reward contract for an individual with challenging behaviour.

Gustav's contract

If I stay in all my lessons without walking away without permission, and attend homework club every Wednesday for eight weeks then I will have a day trip to the seaside with time on the beach, a donkey ride and ice cream.

Signed

Gustav

Importance of positive reinforcement

When positive reinforcement does not occur in your strategies within your care-plan regarding individuals with challenging behaviour you are making your job much much harder. **Positive reinforcement consistently applied supports the individual with challenging behaviour** be more independent, have more life choice and in turn have a better life. A lack of positive reinforcement will allow the negative to be reinforced in the individual with challenging behaviour, causing stress, anxiety and generally a much worse life.

Answer to question 8: Describe how to avoid confrontation with someone who is emotionally agitated.

There are some times in which you will have to communicate with individuals with challenging behaviour who are emotionally agitated. You of course wish to avoid confrontation which will worsen any situation and damage care.

Here are some golden rules to help you avoid confrontation with someone who is emotionally agitated.

1	It may be necessary to **change your tone of voice**, making it quieter so that the individual recognises it as **supportive, encouraging and friendly**.

2	It may be necessary to **acknowledge the individual with challenging behaviour's feelings** and s**how you understand**, and **also provide them with alternative ways to deal with a situation**.

3	It may be necessary to **modify the environment** if it is causing individuals with challenging behaviour to be upset for example the temperature or lighting.

4   It may be necessary to **take a break**, give the individual with challenging behaviour **some time out time to calm down**. Perhaps lead the individual to a quiet area and abandon current activities.

5   It may be necessary to **provide the individual with challenging behaviour with choices** such as where to sit or move to and other activities to do that might take their mind off the problem.

6   It may be necessary **to avoid interrupting individuals** and their behaviour unless there is a safety issue.

7   It may be necessary to **offer a reward** if the individual with challenging behaviour deals with the problem or difficulty that is affecting their behaviour.

8   It may be necessary to **simplify the task** or change your expectations if it is a task that has upset the individual, such as something they are finding too challenging.

9   It may be necessary to **avoid blaming individuals** for their actions.

10   It may be necessary to **try and fulfil any need**, if the situation is caused by having unmet needs.

11   It may be necessary to to **try to provide guidance rather than questioning**, for example 'Let's move in to the other room where's quieter' rather than 'Do you want to go somewhere else?'

12   It may be necessary to **avoid coming across as controlling and dominating**.

13   It may be necessary to **be fair but firm**.

14   It may be necessary to **stay calm and speak slowly and quietly**.

15   It may be necessary to **be patient and set clear expectations**.

16   It may be necessary to **control your communication very carefully** taking care that this does not make the situation worse. **Think about what you say**, your tone of voice, facial expression and body language.

17   It may be necessary to stay at eye level with the individual, do not stand above them if they are sitting. If they don't sit down, remaining standing.

18   It may be necessary to **avoid overcrowding the individual**.

19   It may be necessary to **keep your body relaxed and your facial expression neutral**.

20   It may be necessary to **make sure the situation does not become argumentative**.

21   It may be necessary to **avoid making promises you can't keep**.

Aversive behaviour intervention

Aversive behaviour intervention is an old strategy **which punishes the individual with challenging behaviour in order to suppress or change the challenging behaviour**. Over the last twenty years the focus has changed to use '**non-aversive techniques**' meaning that techniques to **prevent the behaviour happening in the first place should be used**.

Answer to question 9: Describe how using knowledge of the individual can help to manage behaviour that challenges.

It is important for anyone working with or caring for individuals with challenging behaviour that they **understand the individual** to help manage their behaviour. For in that understanding you are better armed to care. It is important to **support and understand their needs**. Understand the individual with challenging behaviour as you do yourself and your care-plan will never be defeated.

In understanding individuals to help manage their behaviour you should have a **person-centred approach** and understand that it is important to recognise the person behind the challenging behaviour to help come up with solutions.

People working with individuals with challenging behaviour should work closely with the individuals **families and carers** as these people can often provide a lot of useful background information about the individual with challenging behaviour. This information leads to a better understanding of the reasons behind the challenging behaviour.

It is also important in the person-centred approach to take into account the feelings, thoughts and views of the individuals with challenging behaviour to encourage decision making and support them in making choices.

Important areas to help staff to support individuals with challenging behaviour

1   The individual with challenging behaviour's history

Something may have happened to the individual with challenging behaviour in the past that may have led to the challenging behaviour they have now, for example fear of a specific person.

2   The individual with challenging behaviour's family and carers

Family members and carers may be more able to support the individual with challenging behaviour and reduce displays of challenging behaviour. **Since family members and carers are most familiar to the individual and may understand them more than you** it is useful to know which family members and carers can best support you in helping the individual with challenging behaviour.

3   **The individual with challenging behaviour's values**.

It is useful to know what the individual with challenging behaviour values are as this can help you form a better relationship with the individual with challenging behaviour. What are the individuals likes and beliefs.

4   **The individual with challenging behaviour's communication needs or difficulties**.

If you are aware of communication difficulties it is best to put strategies in place to find alternative ways of communicating. So that you can reduce the chance of displays of challenging behaviour through communication problems.

5   **The individual with challenging behaviour's medical conditions.**

Recognising any medical conditions of the individual with challenging behaviour can help you support them. Are they in pain or discomfort, is their medical condition becoming a trigger for displays of challenging behaviour. Dealing with the medical problems helps you deal with the patient.

6   **The individual with challenging behaviour's interests or hobbies.**

Knowing about or being interested in an individual with challenging behaviour's hobbies and interests helps you **communicate and bond** with the individual with challenging behaviour. Also it can help distract an individual with challenging behaviour from other things or situations that can trigger displays of challenging behaviour.

7   **The individual with challenging behaviour's likes and dislikes**.

Some individuals with challenging behaviour have very strong dislikes and this may trigger displays of challenging behaviour if the individual is forced to do something they strongly dislike. Also know what an individual with challenging behaviour really likes makes a more effective reward for desired behaviour.

8   **The individual with challenging behaviour's disabilities**.

Has the individual with challenging behaviour any disabilities in addition to their challenging behaviour. Have they autism or mental health issues. Understanding this can help you understand the reasons for their challenging behaviour and find effective help and strategies to help them manage their own behaviour.

How using knowledge of the individual can help to manage behaviour that challenges

John has autism and is hypo-sensitive to touch. His behaviour reflects his need for sensory sensation and he displays this by playing roughly with other children, hugging and gripping people and banging objects.

This behaviour often causes damage to objects and his environment and distress for both children and adults. By understanding his needs and the reasons for his behaviour he can be supported better. The behaviour that challenges can be reduced by providing John sensory stimulation in other ways, such as providing toys that he can hug, grip and bang safely.

Answer to question 10: Describe how to maintain the dignity of individuals when responding to incidents of behaviour that challenges.

When an individual with challenging behaviour displays their challenging behaviour it is important to **maintain their dignity**.

Maintaining the individual with challenging behaviour's dignity

What do we mean when we say **maintain their dignity**. In normal life when something happens beyond our control that is upsetting or embarrassing we would like our friends and family around us to help maintain our dignity and support us. This is even more relevant to individuals with challenging behaviour. **Since that challenging behaviour and it's display's can damage an individuals dignity.** Also for individuals with challenging behaviour **their dignity in this context is in fact their care**. So when we say **maintaining an individual with challenging behaviour's dignity** what we are really saying is **maintaining the individual with challenging behaviour's care**.

To maintain an individual with challenging behaviour's dignity or care you should when responding to incidents of behaviour that challenges:

1   **Avoid shouting, yelling or speaking too loudly**.

2   Give individuals with challenging behaviour **time and space after an incident**; they may not be ready to talk about what happened

3   Try to **calmly explain** what they have done that is not acceptable or desired and point out   some alternative ways of behaving.

4   Understand that individuals with challenging behaviour may not be comfortable making or maintaining eye contact and avoid insisting on this, as it could lead to further incidents of challenging behaviour.

5   **Avoid patronising individuals** with challenging behaviour, treat them as equals.

6   Understand that **extra time may be required** to process information.

7   **Speak clearly and allow time for questions**.

8   Clear up any damage the individual with challenging behaviour has caused during the   incident of challenging behaviour with **as little fuss as possible**.

9   If damage has occurred **avoid any rejection or hostility**.

In a perfect world that is what a professional carer would be, like a good friend or member of the individuals family that's how much they would care.

Answer to question 11: Describe different techniques that are used to defuse behaviour that challenges.

Techniques that are used to diffuse behaviour that challenges are as individual as the individual with challenging behaviour. Such techniques within your care-plan are tailored to each individual with challenging behaviour since such techniques like all of your strategies are **person centred**. Your strategies and these techniques also need to be **consistent**. There needs to be a consistent approach when attempting to diffuse a situation to reduce confusion in the individual with challenging behaviour and reduce the risk of behaviours being learnt in order to get a reward. It is important to use a person-centred approach when dealing with individuals with challenging behaviour and stay calm at all times. You have to make sure that you are not putting yourself at risk when attempting to diffuse challenging behaviour.

Methods of diffusing behaviour that challenges

Methods of diffusing challenging behaviour include **diversion techniques**, **crisis management** and **preventative measures**.

Prevention strategies

Prevention strategies include avoiding certain situations that may trigger displays of challenging behaviour from the individual with challenging behaviour. Prevention strategies are there to **prevent**

displays of challenging behaviour. Prevention strategies are there to **provide routine and structure** to the individual with challenging behaviour. Prevention strategies are finding alternative ways of communicating and pre-planning.

Routine and structure

Some individuals with challenging behaviour display their challenging behaviour more often when there are **changes in their routine and structure**. Individuals with challenging behaviour can find the world and all its accoutrements confusing, and routine and structure give some individuals with challenging behaviour a feeling of **safety and security**. This means that changes in their environment, structure and routine can unsettle the individual.

When introducing individuals with challenging behaviour to new people, places and non-routine events such introduction and path should be done slowly and with patience and support.

Pre-planning

By pre-planning with individuals with challenging behaviour, you can help and support them to manage their behaviour better and avoid incidents of behaviour that challenges.

Major life events

Major changes in an individual with challenging behaviour's life or major life events can lead to behaviour that challenges.

1   Someone moving out of the family home or moving

2   A new job or school

3   Going to a new unknown environment

4 Parents divorcing

5 Going on holiday

Minor life events

Individual's with challenging behaviour can display challenging behaviour even with minor life events and so you must be on your guard and have prevention strategies in place in case of displays of challenging behaviour that can occur due to stress over minor life events by the individual with challenging behaviour. For example:

1 An unexpected visitor coming to their home.

2 A visit by the doctor.

3 Not being able to go to the cinema because the car has broken down.

4 Not being allowed to go to the beach or park due to weather.

Strategies that support individuals with challenging behaviour with changes to routine and structure

Strategies that support individuals with challenging behaviour with changes to routine and structure include:

1 **Plan ahead and prepare** the individual with challenging behaviour for the change, let them know well in advance what is going to happen.

2   **Let the individual with challenging behaviour have familiar items close to them** during the change, for example playing their favourite music, having a book they like, or for a child their favourite toy.

3   **Use visual supports like a visual timetable** to let the individual with challenging behaviour know what will happen at every stage.

4   **Try and keep the same routines** for individuals with challenging behaviour, even if it is a different setting, for example if they have moved to a new care home.

5   **Praise individuals** for coping with the change.

6   **Keep in regular contact** with the people caring for them, or anyone they come into contact with.

7   **Use social stories** to help the individual prepare for the change.

Social stories

Social stories are short descriptions of a particular situation, event or activity, which include specific information about what to expect in that situation and why. They were created by Carol Gray in 1991 to help teach social skills to individuals on the autism spectrum.

Scenarios and strategies

Here are some examples and strategies that you can use to help individuals whose behaviour is caused by changes to routine and structure:

Scenario 1

Bill has to go into care as his ageing parents are no longer able to look after him.

Strategy 1

A **social story** is prepared for Bill to explain what will happen, and how he might feel about the changes. The story should reassure him, showing some of the things in place to help him deal with the change. This may include people who will be there to help him.

Scenario 2

Sarah is about to start a new school, and is anxious about the change to her life and entering an unknown environment.

Strategy 2

Pre-planning will help Sarah to prepare for the changes and will include discussions in advance followed by visits to the new school. She will visit with her parents and teaching assistant first and following the visit will be able to discuss her feelings.

Further visits should be planned to allow Sarah to look at things again and further asses her wants and needs. Once she has time to process the information she has received. This could involve spending more time in areas she feels anxious about, so that she can become more familiar with them.

Pre-planning

Pre-planning is very important in preparing individuals with challenging behaviour for any changes to their routine and structure.

Social story

Here is an example of a prepared social story (pre-plan of desired behaviour) to help a pupil moving to secondary school.

1	In four weeks I will be moving to a new school.

2	The school is very big with lots of people.

3	But that's ok because I will have a teaching assistant to help me Mrs Salon.

4	I will be met at the door everyday by Mrs Salon.

5	I will have to carry a big bag with heavy books.

6	But that's ok because I will be given a locker to keep things in.

7	At lunchtime the dining hall is very busy.

8	But that's ok as Mrs Salon my teaching assistant will take me to lunch every day.

9	If I don't like the dining room I can go to a quiet room to eat my food.

10	There will be lots of different lessons and lots to do during the school day, with lots of different rooms to find.

11	But that's ok as I will have a map with symbols and names of people like Mrs Salon to help me find my way around.

12	My mum will come to school at the end of the day to meet me at the driveway as the street will be very busy with crowds of children.

De-escalation

De-escalation is another technique you can use to diffuse behaviour that challenges. If **prevention techniques** have thus far failed to help the individual with challenging behaviour manage their displays of challenging behaviour you can consider applying de-escalation techniques.

De-escalation techniques

1   **Use appropriate communication skills** for the individual with challenging behaviour. Maybe they don't understand the situation or environment.

2   **Adopt a non-confrontational manner. Keep things simple and keep things positive**. It is no help to the individual with challenging behaviour to turn a drama into a crisis. Confrontation with the individual with challenging behaviour is the last thing you want especially during displays of challenging behaviour.

3   **Use empathy. humanity and care**, the basic foundations of our profession often sadly missed. The big question when displays occur is, **'how would you feel if this had happened to you?'**. Challenging behaviour can be managed, yes, but for some a life sentence. There but for the grace of God go I. Empathy my friend the guide of our care and profession.

4   **Negotiating**. Maybe the display of challenging behaviour is over a desire unfulfilled, maybe some good old reasonableness and common sense can win through.

5   **Minimising threat**. Ideally in the individual with challenging behaviour's life there should be no threat. If a threat presents itself either to or by the individual with challenging behaviour it will be have to be **minimised as soon as possible by all appropriate means**. A threat to or by the individual with challenging behaviour can quickly escalate into something much worse for all parties involved.

6	**Agreeing to any reasonable requests**. Why not? You expect the individual with challenging behaviour to be reasonable and in life we generally get what we want if we are reasonable. Denying reasonable requests breeds frustration and anger leading to a greater frequency of displays of challenging behaviour.

7	**A change of staff member if this would help**. Some individuals with challenging behaviour become familiar and attached to certain staff members, which is actually quite normal if you are giving good care. So if a staff change occurs that is causing problems with the individual with challenging behaviour, a good strategy would be to return the favoured staff member to the individual with challenging behaviour until the trust is there to replace the staff member in question.

8	**Doing nothing or adopting a 'leave and return' strategy if it safe to do so**, for example if the behaviour is not causing harm to the individual or others. Sometimes the best thing to not escalate situations or displays of challenging behaviour is do nothing. Some patients respond best if left alone to calm down.

Distraction techniques

Distraction techniques are other techniques you can use to diffuse behaviour that challenges. Distraction can be an effective way to diffuse behaviour that challenges and thus help individuals with challenging behaviour manage their behaviour by diverting their attention away from their challenging behaviour. Distraction techniques can be a simple and effective way of keeping the individual with challenging behaviour away from danger and reduce their displays of challenging behaviour and it's impacts and effects.

Distraction techniques

1	**Give the individual with challenging behaviour something to do**, such as a puzzle, game or other distracting activity.

2   **Change the scene**, lead them to somewhere else so they are looking at something else, talk about the weather and show them the window so they can have their opinion, or maybe a quick trip to the garden to feed the birds.

3   **Change the conversation or topic** to something the individual with challenging behaviour is interested in.

4   Provide them with a favourite snack or beveridge.

Crisis management

Crisis management techniques are other techniques you can use to diffuse behaviour that challenges. **Crisis management is your last resort of techniques** that you can use to diffuse displays of challenging behaviour. It is your def-com one. What you have left when the challenging behaviour well and truly hits the fan. In some situations it may be necessary. to use physical intervention or administer medication especially if the individual with challenging behaviour or others around them could be harmed, remember Emerson, harming is a no no, otherwise it is the exclusion of common community areas with you.

It is important for staff to be trained in recognising when this is necessary. and to work only within your remit and follow organisational policies. Only staff who are trained are allowed to use physical intervention. Without this training carers can easily not follow policies and procedures and then fall afoul of the law (Human Rights act, Care acts, ect,ect).

Physical Intervention

If you have to use physical intervention:

1   Physical intervention must be carried out by **fully trained and competent staff**.

2   Physical intervention must be **reasonable, necessary and proportionate**.

3   Physical intervention must be **the least restrictive method as possible**.

4   Physical intervention must be used for **the minimum amount of time**.

5   Physical intervention must be **combined with other strategies to de-escalate**.

6   **Physical intervention must be monitored carefully** to identify any signs of medical or   physical distress.

7   Physical intervention must be carried out **only after a rapid risk assessment has been   made although in an emergency situation a formal risk assessment may not be possible**.

8   Physical intervention **must be documented** after the indecent.

It is essential that any staff member undertaking physical interventions understands the law relating to the use of reasonable force. They need to consider:

1   Are there any alternatives to using force?

2   Is it proportionment and necessary?

3   Does it use the least amount of force for the minimum time?

4   Can it be justified in a court of law if necessary?

All organisations that deal with behaviour that challenges must have **clear policies and procedures** for dealing with incidents and **the**

roles and responsibilities of all staff need to be clearly defined. Staff should be clear on what they are allowed and not allowed to do and when they should seek assistance from colleagues, response teams, security and the police.

The Police

The police should only be called as a last resort in situations where:

1　A crime has been committed.

2　All other options to de-escalate have been used, and failed.

3　Serious injury has been sustained.

4　Staff or others are in serious danger.

Defusing a situation

1　Try to **reduce and minimise** the individual with challenging behaviour's levels of distress and anxiety.

2　Use **appropriate communication methods** for the individual with challenging behaviour.

3　**Avoid trying to control the situation**, try to find out from the individual with challenging behaviour what the problem is.

4　Show **compassion and empathy.**

5　**Reassure** the individual with challenging behaviour.

6　Speak clearly and calmly.

7　**Acknowledge their concerns** and feelings and show compassion.

8	Try to **negotiate** with them and work out a reasonable comprimise.

9	**Be honest** with them and don't make promises you can't keep.

10	**Consider staffing needs** if there is a communication breakdown with individual with challenging behaviour.

11	**Encourage positive behaviour** by reinforcing.

12	Avoid taking punitive measures.

13	**Do not embarrass or humiliate** the individual with challenging behaviour, unlike CastleBeck Care.

14	**Remove yourself from the situation if appropriate**, saying "I'll just leave you for a while".

15	Use a **friendly** tone.

16	**Smile**.

17	**Acknowledge** what they are saying by nodding.

18	Use a **non-threatening** stance and posture.

19	Avoid making sudden movements.

20	Allow personal space.

21	Use touch if appropriate to show **reassurance and affection**.

Possible reasons for challenging behaviour and possible strategies

Challenging behaviour:	**Biting**

Possible reasons

1. Toothache or mouth pain (sores, blisters etc).
2. Seeking sensory input.
3. A reaction to something upsetting or stressful in the environment.
4. Seeking attention.
5. Frustration or distress about not being able to communicate something.
6. Frustration at their inability to get their needs met.

Possible strategies

1. Have medical reasons investigated to make sure there is no pain or dental problems.
2. Provide alternative items to bite to provide sensory input.
3. Provide the individual with challenging behaviour with structured activities.
4. Provide a relaxed environment and look for triggers which cause anxiety or distress so these can be minimised.
5. Use effective communication and reinforce the fact that biting is not acceptable or a desired behaviour. Some individuals with challenging behaviour may need visual supports, such as a no biting symbol.

Challenging behaviour: **Hitting out or kicking**

Possible reasons

1. Being hypersensitive to noise, smells, touch, sight or crowds and becoming distressed at these.
2. Frustration at being unable to communicate.
3. Meeting unfamiliar people.
4. Being unwell, uncomfortable or in pain.
5. Changes to routine and structure.
6. Not wanting to do something, such as getting dressed in certain clothes or taking part in particular activities.
7. Seeking sensory input if they are hypo-sensitive.

Possible strategies

1. Create an appropriate environment which will not cause them distress, such as blocking out noise or using low impact lighting.
2. Reward appropriate behaviour.
3. Provide alternative, more appropriate activities.
4. Prepare them for new events or experiences and meeting new people with photographs and social stories.
5. For hypo-sensitive individuals provide alternatives for sensory stimulation, such as kicking or hitting a punch bag or games or songs involving hand clapping.

Story Builder

To help diffuse behaviour that challenges you can use 'Story Builder' a computer based tool that can be used to create individualised stories and is used with autistic individuals. It was developed by Ruth Evans and Davis Moore and allows the user to build a computerised step-by-step story. This can be used to prepare individuals with challenging behaviour for events and changes in their lives which they may find stressful and could result in challenging behaviour.

Answer to question 12: Explain how your own actions can diffuse or exacerbate an individual's behaviour.

You the carer can affect both positively and negatively an individual with challenging behaviour, **depending on the quality of your care**.

You can diffuse or exacerbate challenging behaviour by an individual when it is displayed.

Actions that can exacerbate displays of challenging behaviours:

1. Being threatening or threatening behaviour.
2. Using sarcasm.
3. Causing humiliation.
4. Using humour inappropriately or if it can be negatively misunderstood.
5. Making the individual with challenging behaviour feel cornered or hemmed in, or standing too close to them, invading their body space.
6. Talking over them or interrupting them.
7. Not listening to the individual.
8. Blaming them.
9. Showing that you are agitated, or any display of negative behaviour on your part.
10. Shouting or being loud.
11. Threatening body language. Raised fists etc.
12. Raising your eyebrows (This can indicate you do not believe the individual or are alarmed/surprised by their actions.)
13. Forcing them to make eye-contact and saying things like 'don't be rude, look at me when I'm talking to you'.
14. Laughing at them or at their expense. Humiliating them.
15. Over challenging them by asking them to fulfil tasks when it is difficult for them to do as you have asked.
16. Showing them that you are upset, which can make them more stressed.
17. Sighing, yawning or looking fed up.
18. Failing to respect their privacy, such as entering their room without knocking.
19. Making sudden movements, grabbing, gripping them.
20. Joining in an argument they are having with someone.

The above actions and others like it can exacerbate displays of challenging behaviour (**make it worse**) or even be a trigger to it's displays. The message is simple **don't do the above unless you want to make the displays of challenging behaviour a whole lot worse**. The above actions show something incredibly clearly. **A carer who did such things would be seen as a very bad carer indeed**. Back to the horror story, force, humiliation, sarcastic, impatient, bored, angry, a perfect recipe for a terrible carer.

Actions that can diffuse displays of challenging behaviours

1. Staying calm.
2. Allowing the individual enough personal space.
3. Avoiding raising your voice and thinking about your tone.
4. Not embarrassing them in front of others.
5. Empathising with them, showing you understand what they are saying.
6. Giving them choices to make it easy to do what you are asking them to do.
7. Thinking carefully about body language and avoid clenching your fists or other signs of agitation.
8. Not forcing eye contact as individuals with challenging behaviour may be uncomfortable with this.
9. Avoid signs of laughing or giggling.
10. Control your breathing, if you begin to breath heavy the individual with challenging behaviour may think you are getting angry or agitated.
11. Talking about something else than the display of challenging behaviour to distract the individual.
12. Changing the subject.
13. Acknowledging the individual with challenging behaviour's feelings.
14. Being aware of your own mood and actions and making sure how you are feeling does not affect the way you treat someone.
15. Try to provide a quiet place to discuss the situation if needed.

The importance of diffusing or exacerbating individuals with challenging behaviour

Two extreme cases of abuse developed in two care homes in Devon. The staff were accused of several offences against individuals with challenging behaviour who were in their care. With imprisonment of the patients in empty rooms for very long periods as **'punishment'** as a strategy to control challenging behaviour.

The prosecutor at court described the care homes as **'organised and systemic abuse'** and the training was **'at best outdated at worst criminal'**. The jury were told that individuals with challenging behaviour were imprisoned in isolation rooms as if they **'were badly behaved animals'**. Andrew Langon QC stated 'The view was taken that the residents had somehow learnt to behave badly and that behaviour had to be unlearnt. If they were kept in isolation rooms long enough they would learn a lesson and change their behaviour'. Strangely the same sort of ideas and attitudes of the Victorians and not so strangely attitudes and actions that goes against all our current principles of care, hence the trouble these care homes and their staff are in.

The heart of this example is a lot of the rot was caused by unbelievable ignorance and **misunderstanding of individuals with challenging behaviour**. Patients were punished if they:

1   **Stared at a staff member.**

Have you ever been to a mental hospital. The patients stare at you all the time for a million and one reasons. Individuals with challenging behaviour may be bored and you are new, or you asked them a question so they stare at you to understand you, they may be thinking of upcoming lunch and staring in your general direction. Half of the residents were probably isolated for that 'crime'. Ah yes one last thing **it's not illegal to stare,** so you can't legally stop individuals with challenging behaviour from staring at whatever they like.

2   **Facial twitches**

Another feeble excuse for isolation. Some individuals with challenging behaviour cannot control their face muscles, others are probably **reacting in fear** that yes the carer is the one who enjoys isolating you. So no twitching!

3   **Asking questions repeatedly**

Many individuals with challenging behaviour have communication difficulties added the extra stress of being isolated for not correctly carrying out orders you ask again to be sure and receive more isolation, nice! The prosecutor was wrong, animals get better treatment than these poor patients.

4   **Missing a hair appointment**

Like WTF! An individual with challenging behaviour misses a hair appointment and receives isolation, maybe the individual couldn't make it because they were already locked up in isolation.

It's the patients hair and the patients appointment, **it is not a crime to miss a hair appointment**, and **where is the empathy**. It's an individual with challenging behaviour, life is far from a perfect Swiss clock, things change all the time. I got it wrong previously there are animals in those care homes unfortunately it is the carers.

I previously stated that the to the road to hell is paved in good intentions, but in this case the road is paved in diabolic intentions and went to the depths at a hundred miles an hour heading west.

To the patients, a terrible experience that no doubt exacerbated their challenging behaviour to such a degree that they were probably traumatised and mentally scarred after the experience. Two care homes turned into prisons crossed with concentration camps full of 'badly behaved animals'.
An extreme but educational example of how the actions of the carers exacerbated the individual's challenging behaviour.

Answer to question 13: Describe referral services available to provide support for individuals.

There are a number of various specialist services available to provide support for individuals with challenging behaviour.

Speech and language therapist (SLT)

Speech and language therapists (SLTs) are specially trained members of staff who work with diagnostic and educational teams to provide comprehensive language, communication and speech assessments for individuals with challenging behaviour who have communication difficulties.

SLTs who provide therapy for individuals with challenging behaviour who have speech and language disorders do so in small group sessions or work in partnership with teachers or in consultation with parents.

A speech and language therapists role includes:

1	Forming plans for support for alternative methods of communication (for example sign language lessons, or teaching Makaton) for those who do not use spoken language.

2	Building on receptive and expressive language skills for those with developing language.

3	Working on the more subtle aspects of conversation with those with high verbal skills.

4	Looking at the more subtle aspects of pragmatics, and conversational reciprocity which will be the focus.

5	Training staff members in how to better communicate and diffuse displays of challenging behaviour through appropriate communication methods and techniques.

Psychiatrist

A psychiatrist is your Dr Freud, a helpful medical doctor specialising in mental health issues such as anxiety, depression, personality disorders and addictions. In short lots of challenging behaviour! Oh yes!

Psychiatrists may be involved when there are cases of mental health problems which result in behaviour that challenges and can offer follow-up treatment and interventions.

Paediatrician

Paediatricians are specialist who work exclusively with children, especially their health and development and any developmental disorders. They deal with everything from verrucas to dyslexia to more serious challenges as childhood autism and other conditions that can be a cause of challenging behaviour. Like psychiatrists paediatricians will be involved in follow up treatments and interventions where necessary.

Clinical Psychologist

Clinical psychologist are trained staff members that focus on the challenging behaviour and how it affects the individual, they often produce a behaviour management plan.

Doctor

Yes your good old general practitioner (GP), on top of recommending paracetamol for any ailment the GP is often the first point of contact for the individual with challenging behaviour, who then refers the individual for more specialised care, such as a paediatrician or psychiatrist.

Doctors of all calibres can prescribe medication for the treatment of symptoms that can lead to challenging behaviour for example Ritalin, which helps decrease impulsivity and hyperactivity. Anxiety, depression or obsessive-compulsive disorder can be first treated with medication prescribed by the GP.

Counsellor

Individuals with challenging behaviour often experience anxiety when dealing with changes and life's uncertainties. Change of school, home life, job ect. Counsellors can help in such situations by helpfully talking through issues. Some counsellors are trained in cognitive behavioural therapy (CBT) which can help an individual with challenging behaviour think about themselves and other people with the aim of helping them to function better in day-to-day life.

Counsellors can also apply behavioural or educational interventions to help the individual with challenging behaviour, using highly structured and intensive training sessions to help individuals with challenging behaviour develop social interaction and communication skills.

There is also family counselling for the parents and siblings of individuals with challenging behaviour to help families cope with living with the displays of challenging behaviour.

Educational psychologists

Educational psychologists are specially trained staff usually at school or university environments that help individuals with challenging behaviour. They carry out assessments and look at the learning profiles and needs of the individual with challenging behaviour. They offer expert advice to parents and teachers and the individual with challenging behaviour, to improve their chances of education.

Social worker or care manager

Social workers and care managers assess the care needs of individuals with challenging behaviours, and their families. They also arrange services such as healthcare, to meet those needs.

Behaviour support team

Behaviour support teams supports families with individuals with challenging behaviour who display behaviour that challenges. The team plan and introduce behaviour management programmes. An individual with challenging behaviour and/or their family can be referred to the behaviour and support team by a GP, social worker or school.

Outreach worker

An outreach worker helps the individual with challenging behaviour to access opportunities and activities outside their home, such as education, sport or hobbies. For example a drama therapist or drama therapy. Nothing feeds the soul of the individual with challenging behaviour than a little Shakespeare.

Occupational therapists

Occupational therapists assess the difficulties individuals with challenging behaviour have with day-to-day activities and help them overcome these difficulties, promoting independence and activities which they might be able to assess and provide support.

Social participation, structured rest and sleep, taking part in education and employment and exploring play. I assume occupational therapists were thin on the ground in Devon with patients being put in isolation for missing a hair appointment.

Physiotherapist

As the mind needs therapy so does the body. Physiotherapists are specially trained staff to deal with good health and the recovery of the individual with challenging behaviour after injury or through ill health such as a stroke, car accident, or head injuries from a fall etc.

Answer to question 14: Describe your own limitations and accountabilities when supporting individuals exhibiting behaviour that is perceived as challenging.

Hospitals, care homes, and other professional organisations have written polices and procedures that cover the limits of your authority and accountability when dealing with individuals with challenging behaviour within that organisation.

Policies and procedures

Your organisation. will have written guidelines on preventing, responding to and managing individuals with challenging behaviour. There will be ongoing staff training on how to manage behaviour that challenges.

Dealing with challenging behaviour can be very stressful and can have a negative effect on staff well-being and may even lead to injury. It is important especially within your organisations polices and procedures to support staff, especially if the staff are placed in stressful situations.

Staff support

It is important that staff know when to seek additional support and are clear on how to access this support. Staff need to know their limitations within their role and understand it's ok to ask for help within their role and how to do so efficiently. Staff also need to have a clear understanding of the roles of colleagues within the organisation and which issues need to be referred or escalated to. Staff also need to know when they are able to work alone and when there should be more than one staff member present.

Physical restraint

In cases of physical restraint, the organisational policies (polices and procedures)must be followed and the staff must be aware of them. Only staff who are correctly trained and authorised to restrain should do so for safety reasons. If restraint is used correct documentation must be completed and staff must be familiar with recording and reporting procedures.

Physical restraint should only be used as a last resort and only by staff authorised and trained to so so.

Reasons for physical restraint

1   To stop someone being injured (as per Emerson).

2   Because someone needs urgent medical help or intervention and the individual with challenging behaviour does not have the mental capacity to agree to the medical help.

Staff must also be aware and understand what 'mental capacity' is under the mental capacity act.

Staff protection

Organisations must ensure that staff know how to protect themselves by:

1   Avoid being in an individual with challenging behaviour's personal space.

2   Avoid small enclosed spaces.

3   Keep if possible a physical barrier between staff and the individual with challenging   behaviour for example a desk.

4   Make staff aware of the nearest exits from a dangerous situation.

Staff need to be aware of the policies and procedures on reporting incidents and information to others, including family and staff, and other appropriate agencies and be aware of issues of confidentiality.

Legal considerations

Your organisations staff must be aware as per the policies and procedures and various legal acts of the legal consequences to their actions when working with individuals with challenging behaviour and be aware of the current legislation to protect individuals with challenging behaviour.

Current legislation that protects individuals with challenging behaviour

1   Human Rights Act 1998.
2   Mental Capacity Act 2005.
3   Mental Health Act 2007.
4   Deprivation of Liberty Safeguards (DoLS).
5   Care Act 2014.
6   Safeguarding of Vulnerable Adults Act 2006.

A good example of an organisation not taking legal considerations as applied by the above acts is the Winterbourne abuse case.

Ethical considerations

Everybody must comply with the Human Rights Act 1998. The act covers ethical considerations which must be legally considered when dealing with individuals with challenging behaviour.

1   Treat the individual with challenging behaviour with kindness, dignity and compassion.

2   Work in the individual with challenging behaviour's best interests.
3   Balance safety from harm and freedom of choice especially with those without full mental capacity.
4   Involve the individual with challenging behaviour in decisions about their care and support.
5   Provide advocacy for individuals with challenging behaviour who need it.
6   Show understanding of the individual with challenging behaviour and help them improve their quality of life.
7   Foster and support positive relationships between individuals and the people who provide care and support.

Education settings

In an educational setting or organisation. their policies and procedures state that challenging behaviour is any behaviour which:

1   Challenges the everyday smooth running of the school.
2   Interferes with a pupils learning.
3   Interferes with the learning of other pupils.
4   Puts staff or pupils at risk.
5   Prevents the environment being safe and orderly.
6   Is less responsive to the school's usual interventions for misbehaviour.
7   Has a duration, intensity, frequency or persistence that is beyond the normal range of what   the school tolerates.

Answer to question 15: Describe how to report incidents of behaviour that is challenging.

Incidents of behaviour is recorded for a large number of reasons, to aid in the health care of the individual, clues for triggers within your support strategies, reactions to new medications, for information purposes etc. They are recorded to help us understand why the behaviours occur and to measure the effectiveness of the support provided.

Reporting incidents of challenging behaviour

According to your organisations policies and procedures you will have a set form to fill in after each incident of challenging behaviour. Every organisation has an agreed criteria on what constitutes an incident. If you are not sure what constitutes an incident of challenging behaviour that requires a report you need to speak to your team leader or line manager.

You need to record what happened and if restraint was used. A copy of this documentation should be placed on the individuals file for future reference and other copies may need to be sent to relevant agencies.

Your reports are used to reduce the likelihood of similar incidents happening in the future by identifying patterns and possible triggers for your support strategies.

Risk assessment documentation

As well as reporting on incidents of challenging behaviour you may also have to fill in risk assessment documentation to protect the individual with challenging behaviour and others from harm in the future.

A risk assessment is usually made after a physical intervention has taken place as part of your report.

After a physical intervention has occurred a written record should be completed which should include the following:

1. Name of the individual with challenging behaviour.

2. Date, time, and location.

3. Description of the behaviour that led to the use of restraint.

4. Type of restraint used.

5. Duration of the restraint.

6. Names of the staff involved.

7. The effectiveness of the restraint.

8. Any consequences.

Accident forms

As well as reporting any incidents of challenging behaviour you may as a professional carer need to fill in an accident form on behalf of the individual with challenging behaviour in addition to a risk assessment as well as check whether the incident needs reporting under the Reporting of Injuries, Disease and Dangerous Occurrences Regulation (RIDDOR) 1995.

ABC Chart

Our old friend the ABC chart (**Antecedent-Behaviour-Consequence**) is a useful method to identifying triggers, patterns of behaviour and how to deal with displays of challenging behaviour. Your reports of incidents of challenging behaviour help to make the ABC chart more effective at identifying patterns and triggers.

Antecedent

The event that occurred before the display of challenging behaviour.

Write down what happened before the display of challenging behaviour started. Who was present, what was the individual with challenging behaviour was doing, where were they.

Behaviour

What was the behaviour that you observed during the display of challenging behaviour, describe in detail.

Consequence

What happened after the display of challenging behaviour and as a result of it.

Continuous ABC recording

It may be necessary for some individuals with challenging behaviour to give them continuous ABC recording to consider all possible triggers, which have been worked out from previous assessments, that occur within a particular period of time, for example just after the emergency admission of an individual with serious psychiatric problems. This helps to identify the likelihood of an incidents occurring under specific conditions.

Continuous ABC Form

Here is a basic example of a continuous ABC form.

Individual's name:

Date:

Start time:

Stop time:

Staff member observing:

Triggers:	Behaviour:
Outcomes:	
Left alone	Verbal abusing
Provided with attention	
Activity cancelled	
New activity started	
Given an instruction	Physical aggression
Stop task	
Others receiving attention:	
Presence of other people:	

Narrative ABC recording

Narrative ABC recording is an ABC chart that is designed to tell a story of what is happening with an individuals behaviour by writing accounts of the events or narrative of the events. Narrative ABC recording can be the best way of understanding incidents. Narrative ABC charts enable certain information to be analysed including:

1. Dates, times and location associated with behaviour that challenges.
2. People present who may trigger behaviour that challenges.
3. The frequency of the behaviours.
4. The range of behaviours seen.
5. The impact of different types of behaviour.

Narrative ABC record chart

Individual's name: Location:

Staff present:

Date: Time started:

Time finished:

Triggers:

Describe the action of the individual:

Describe the factors that contributed to the behaviour:
(e.g. environment, people, change of routine)

Outcomes:

Describe what happened after the behaviour:

Impact:

Describe the result of the behaviour:

Links to other incidents:

Was this incident linked to any other episodes of challenging behaviour.

Completed by:

Scatter plots

Scatter plots are a way to record incidents of challenging behaviour and is used when the behaviour is most likely to occur. In the Scatter plot document the day is split into blocks of time, for examples every 30 minutes, and can focus on behaviour that challenges in three ways, verbal abuse, physical aggression and self-injury. Although scatter plot records can focus on any challenging behaviour.

Self-monitoring

The person who knows how their challenging behaviour feels the best is the individual themselves, and in progressing with more involvement of the **individual in their own care** there is the **Self-monitoring document** should an individual with challenging behaviour have the capability and if it is within their best interests. Self-monitoring can show the individuals mood or feelings throughout the day to help direct the ABC chart.

Answer to question 16: Describe how reflection on an incident can assist in managing future behaviour.

To reflect. To look to past events and consider them, understand them, to learn their lessons of regret and thus avoid the negative and continue with the positive. During and following a display of challenging behaviour, the impacts and effects to the feelings of those dealing with the challenging behaviour are felt. It is important to recognise this, and as part of your strategies to help the individual with challenging behaviour manage their own behaviour to use reflection of past events of incidents of challenging behaviour to help you help them.

The key to this is to recognise that these situations do happen and for staff not to take things personally. After all if the individual with challenging behaviour could easily control their behaviour there would be no need for us. Staff members must recognise that they have their own limitations and should not be afraid of seeking support. Saying this it is easy for a carer to receive negative impacts upon their feelings when dealing with individuals with challenging behaviour which is the way reflection of past events can help the staff member to deal with these impacts and avoid any future effects. This can assist the staff member mange future incidents of challenging behaviour.

Negative feelings after an incident of challenging behaviour include:

1. Anger
2. Rage
3. Fear
4. Disappointment
5. Shock

6   Failure

7   Guilt

By reflecting on incidents of challenging behaviour we can look at what happened and consider the reasons for the behaviour and once a conclusion is reached how the indecent of challenging behaviour can be avoided in the future. We also can look at the way the incident was dealt with and if the management of the incident can be improved. Reflection allows us to study the consequences of the incident and whether it was dealt with effectively, did the incident de-escalate and why or did an intervention exacerbate the incident? All of this information can help us deal with the behaviour in the future.

Every individual is different and reflection allows us to help understand that individual, their needs and abilities, there reactions to situations and their likes and dislikes. We as staff get to know personally our charges. From such knowledge we can avoid past mistakes and have the ability to provide better care. As they say hindsight is twenty twenty.

The reflective cycle

The reflective cycle (Gibbs 1988) is a useful process to follow to encourage you the staff member to think, analyse and reflect upon incidents of challenging behaviour to assist you and others in managing incidents of challenging behaviour.

1   Description

What happened?

2	Feelings

What were every bodies thoughts and feelings especially the individual with challenging behaviour?

3	Evaluation

What was positive and what was negative about the experience?

4	Analysis

What sense can you make of the situation?

5	Conclusion

What else could have been done?

6	Action planning

Upon reflection what should be done again?

Some useful questions to asked when reflecting upon incidents of challenging behaviour to help you manage that behaviour.

1	What caused the behaviour?

2	What was the situation that led up to it?

3	What feelings were involved?

4	What was the solution?

5	What were the consequences?

6	How did the individual feel? How did you feel?

7	What were the alternative actions available?

8	How well did you do?

9   Are you satisfied with the action you took and how you dealt with it?

10   What could you do differently next time?

Answer to question 17: Describe how your own reactions can affect behaviour that challenges.

It is off course important to manage your own feelings when deal with individuals with challenging behaviour, and be aware of how your own actions and reactions can affect the individuals with challenging behaviour you are caring for. Your actions and reactions can de-escalate a situation and calm the individual down but can also make things a whole lot worse.

Reactions that can help de-escalate

1   Remain calm

2   Speak quietly

3   Listening

4   Avoiding becoming involved in an argument or debate

Reactions that could exacerbate

1   Arguing

2   Shouting

3   Patronising

4   Belittling them by dismissing their feelings by using phrases like 'calm down', 'you shouldn't feel that way,' it'll be ok'.

5   Showing your anger.

Lowering stress in staffing

A 2009 study by Thomas and Rose found that staff under stress were likely to respond negatively to challenging behaviour because of course they would be under the limits of their patience. If you reduce stress to the staff from challenging behaviour you will in turn be able to produce better care which ultimately is in the individual with challenging behaviour's best interests.

Answer to question 18: Describe the possible consequences of your own actions in dealing with behaviour that challenges.

When working and caring for individuals with challenging behaviour we have to look at our role and the consequences of our own actions. A great deal of care goes into giving good care, we need to help minimise undesirable behaviour by avoiding causing unnecessary stress and anxiety and help create a calm environment.

Some things we can do to help the individual with challenging behaviour include:

1   Be patient and explain things clearly, understanding that they may need extra time to process information and that they may need to ask lots of questions for clarification.

2   Don't expect the individual with challenging behaviour to make eye contact as this can make some individuals uncomfortable and could cause anxiety and exacerbate their behaviour.

3   Understand that the individual with challenging behaviour is not being rude or trying to offend if they are being frank and honest.

4   Value the individual with challenging behaviour.

5   Do not touch them without warning or by surprise as this could make the individual jump or be uneasy.

The consequences of your actions

Not being patient, forcing eye contact, reacting poorly, treating the individual as valueless and touching the individual with challenging behaviour can exacerbate their challenging behaviour and can trigger displays of challenging behaviour.

Your own actions could be a trigger for behaviour that challenges or make incidents worse.

Actions not to do:

1   Do not try to hug an individual with challenging behaviour if they have issues with being   touched.

2   Do not shout at an individual with challenging behaviour or try to talk over them, in order to stop them shouting.

3   Do not use sarcasm.

Negative actions

Here are some actions that can be taken that would lead to increased anxiety or trigger displays of challenging behaviour.

1   'Now calm down and stop being silly'.

This statement could make the individual with challenging behaviour feel like a child and also degrades their condition or behaviour to something 'silly'. A patient with dementia does not think their dementia is silly.

2   'Look at me when I'm talking to you don't be so rude'.

Forcing an individual with challenging behaviour to look at you can trigger displays of challenging behaviour through stressing the individual.

3   'Just shut up. I'm sick of listening to you.'

Shutting up the individual with challenging behaviour can cause a display of challenging behaviour through belittling them and frustration at being unable to communicate. Also saying you are sick of listening to them puts across that you, the carer, do not want to listen to the individual with challenging behaviour and therefore why communicate.

Answer to question 19: Describe how to support individuals to understand their behaviour in terms of:

Events and feeling's leading up to it:

Many individuals with challenging behaviour struggle to understand their own feelings and emotions through such things as their condition, their age, their emotional state, their mental capabilities and facilities, their maturity etc. This struggle can cause displays of challenging behaviour as the individual. may be using the displays to understand their feelings and communicate those feelings and emotions. It may be they do not want or cannot communicate verbally and so use their displays of challenging behaviour as a more immediate and direct route for the individual to get their message across.

Actions that prevent the individual communicating verbally

1	The individual cannot communicate verbally and must resort to non-verbal communication.

2	The individual may have limited skills or poor communication.

3	The individual may become inarticulate when in a stressful situation.

4	The individual may freeze or stutter when in a stressful situation.

Understanding emotions and feelings can be difficult for most individuals with challenging behaviour, especially those with dementia, autism or learning disabilities, but by helping the individual with challenging behaviour understand their feelings and emotions, we can help the individual with challenging behaviour understand **why** they feel that way. With that **why** it is easier to treat individuals and help them manage their challenging behaviour because they themselves will understand their conditions better.

Strategies to help individuals understand their feelings and emotions

1	Talk to the individual with challenging behaviour when they are calm and relaxed, about their views, what was their thoughts, emotions and feelings on particular events in the past or possible challenges in the future.

2   Social stories, comic strip conversations and other visual aids can be used if verbal communication is difficult.

3   An anxiety diary can be kept to help identify their feelings and put strategies in place to cope with them.

Their actions:

Individuals with challenging behaviour need to understand what behaviour and actions are acceptable and which are unacceptable for various reasons. Once the individual with challenging behaviour understands this fundamental base they will be well on the way to a much better quality of life. They can manage their emotions and feelings better, and develop more self-control. With this improved self-control they can make better progress managing their own behaviour.

The consequences of their behaviour:

Everything in life has a consequence either good or bad depending on your view. Many individuals with challenging behaviour cannot or wish not to see the consequences of their actions. The results of their displays of challenging behaviour. Many do not have a clear understanding of how the world works. The world is challenging and confusing. Individuals need to have an informed choice regarding the consequences of their actions. They need to be told and understand what could happen if they display challenging behaviour or perform unacceptable actions. This gives the individual with challenging behaviour an opportunity to learn.

If the individual is displaying challenging behaviour the individual should be given a **pre-warning** to help the individual **understand the consequences** of their actions. It also allows the individual to redirect themselves and should they keep their self-control should be rewarded. Any consequences need to make sense and be understood by the individual. Also behaviour needs to be treated consistently to help the individual learn the consequences of their actions and have consistent opportunity to apply self-control.

If the consequences to unacceptable actions are not clearly communicated to the individual regarding their display of challenging behaviour the individual with challenging behaviour will not understand the link between their actions and the consequences and will not have the opportunity to learn from their mistakes.

Some golden rules to help individuals with challenging behaviour understand the consequences of their behaviour:

1	Use clear, concise and appropriate language so the individual with challenging behaviour can understand what they are being told.

2	Give the individual with challenging behaviour clear and reasonable expectations for appropriate behaviour.

3	Link the consequences to the display of challenging behaviour so the individual can understand the link.

4	Allow the individual with challenging behaviour informed choices. Tell them what will happen if they choose appropriate behaviour or inappropriate behaviour.

5	Use positive reinforcement for appropriate behaviour and look for opportunities to notice when an individual displays desired behaviour.

6	Be consistent with your strategies and expectations in case the individual tests your consistency by displaying the behaviour multiple times to see your reactions.

7	Keep calm and carry on!

Documentation to help the individual manage their behaviour

There are plenty of forms and documentation that help the individual with challenging behaviour understand their challenging behaviour, understand what are the triggers to displays of challenging behaviour and understand the consequences of their actions.

Behaviour Reflection Chart

Name:

Description of behaviour:

Why I behaved in this way:

The consequences of my behaviour:

How I can change my behaviour:

Behaviour Improvement Report

Name:

This is the behaviour that is not acceptable:

Shouting out:

Talking when others are speaking:

Being rude to others:

Being unkind to others:

Name calling:

Distracting others:

Ruining games for other people:

Spoiling the work of others:

Throwing things:

Interrupting:

Being silly:

Refusing to do as you are asked:

Not keeping your hands to yourself:

Comments:

Staff:

Individual:

Signatures:

Answer to question 20: Identify a range of support services available to those involved in episodes of behaviour that challenges:

It is not just the individual with challenging behaviour that needs support and care. The stress of caring for someone else can lead to stress. There are a number of support services available for both the individual with challenging behaviour and their carers.

Requesting a needs assessments

Families of individuals with challenging behaviour can request a needs assessment from their local authority who will assess the needs of the individual and if necessary put support in place to meet those needs. Examples of the local authority support:

1	Respite care.
2	Professionals who can visit the family home.
3	Support of the family with behaviour issues.
4	Information sheet called 'Social services: getting help for your child'.
5	Carers direct helpline 0300 123 1053.

Carers helpline

The carers helpline provides advice on all aspects of caring, such as benefits, individual budgets, time off, leaving and returning to work or education.

Counselling

A GP can refer individuals and their families to a counsellor, this is available on the NHS or privately. For individuals with autism there is the Autism helpline (0808 800 4104) which has a list of counsellors who understand ASD. They can offer support and advice for parents, children and siblings.

Support groups

Support groups are available around the country and it can be useful to talk to people in similar situations to communicate and discus problems and share useful coping strategies and behaviour management.

Behaviour teams

Some local authorities have behaviour teams that advise and support by carrying out assessments and preparing behaviour support plans for individuals with challenging behaviour to help with their problems and needs. There is also outreach teams and other professionals for example occupational therapists, who can support the individuals with challenging behaviour.

Benefits

Carers may be able to receive benefits such as Carer's Allowance. This could help to provide finances to employ extra help that will give the carer some free time for themselves.

Taking time and a network of care

Taking a break reduces stress and is important for the carers and individuals health, also a network of family and friends can share the load of care.

Home care

Some local authorities offer home support to the care of individuals with challenging behaviour.

Looking after your healthcare

A GP can provide support and refer you to appropriate services.

Effects of challenging behaviour upon carers and staffing

Working with individuals with challenging behaviour is stressful and can cause health concerns, this stress and health concerns are vastly increased with dealing with individuals with violent and aggressive challenging behaviour.

Negative effects of dealing with violent and abusive individuals

1. Low motivation.

2. Low staff morale.

3. Poor retention of staff.

4. High stress levels leading to a degradation of care.

5. High absenteeism.

All in all a lot of staff problems, because of this employers should make sure there is sufficient support for those dealing with individuals with challenging behaviour. It is important for staff to have the right training so that they will be better equipped to deal with the stress.

Staff training

Staff should be trained to develop de-escalation techniques and physical breakaway methods. Some organizations have systems of internal coaches and mentors to support newer and less-experienced staff, especially those who have not worked with challenging behaviour before. Some organisations use buddying schemes where an experienced member of staff works with a less experienced member of staff to show them the ropes.

It is important that there are clear guidelines and policies for staff to follow and that they know how to deal with incidents of challenging behaviour and what to report and to whom. Every organisation. should have a preventative approach to managing violence and abuse resulting from challenging behaviour and an 'open door' culture should be encouraged where issues are shared and discussed.

What to do following an incident of challenging behaviour

Following an incident of challenging behaviour it is important that staff are supported and that a formal debrief should take place along with a review of risk assessment and risk management. Staff can be helped through a process of reflection to try to identify triggers and how future incidents can be reduced.

Legal implications

It is not just a case of **should** employers be supporting staff it is also a case of employers **must** support staff through the law. Employers like staff have a duty of care, employers have a legal duty to protect staff from physical harm. **The Health and Safety at Work Act 1974** states that employers have a duty, as far as is reasonably practicable, to ensure the health, safety and welfare of their employees while at work. **The Reporting of Injuries, diseases and Dangerous Occurrences Regulations 1995** require employers to notify their enforcing authority in the event of an accident at work that results in death, serious injury or incapacity of normal duties at work for seven days or more.

Social Care Institute for Excellence (SCIE)

The Social Care Institute for Excellence (SCIE) provides practice guidance for employers of care workers stating that they should:

1	Ensure staff are provided with the training they need to do their job well.

2	Ensure care workers are supported by other professionals who can provide practical and emotional support.

3	Ensure that abuse of care workers is taken seriously and that training is in place that supports workers to understand and respond to challenging behaviour.

4	Ensure workers do not feel isolated.

5	Involve care workers in day-to-day decision-making.

6	Provide strong leadership, regular supervision and ongoing practical and emotional support to front line care staff.

Organisational policies to support staff who work with individuals with challenging behaviour

Organisations should have policies to support staff who work with individuals with challenging behaviour which should include:

1	Risk assessment

2	How incidents are reported

3	Lone working

4   Bullying and harassment

5   Health and safety

6   Physical intervention policy

7   Dealing with violence

An online survey carried out by Cairncross and Kitson (2013) found that the most common ways staff felt they were supported after incidents of challenging behaviour where:

1   Management debrief.

2   Supervision.

3   Training.

4   Counselling.

5   Mentoring.

6   Legal advice.

Under-reporting of violence and abuse

There is a danger that many cases of abuse and violence to staff go unreported hence an open door policy should be in force within your orginisation. Many cases of abuse and violence towards staff goes unreported because of:

1   Avoiding paperwork that would have resulted in the reporting of the event or incident.

2   Staff being unclear of the reporting procedure and next steps following an indecent.

3   Violence and abuse being viewed as part of the job.

4   Staff not being clear about what constitutes violence and abuse.

5   Staff feeling it would reflect badly upon them and that others may feel they are   incompetent.

6   Staff feeling they will be blamed.

7   Staff being more 'tolerant' and 'understanding' of the abuse as it may be seen as part of the   individual's condition.

Answer to question 21: Describe support systems available to maintain own well-being:

Since injury and health issues can result from stress in working in an environment caring for individuals with challenging behaviour, maintaining your own health and well-being is paramount.
Your employer has a duty of care to you, **but you yourself have a duty of caring for yourself**. Stress is the most common problem within the profession and the health issues it causes includes:

1   Gastrointestinal problems
2   Headaches
3   Back pain
4   Disturbed sleep
5   High blood pressures

6	Alcohol and drug dependency
7	Heart disease

The Health and Safety Executive (HSE) defines stress as '**the adverse reaction people have to excessive pressures or other types of demand placed on them**'.

Common causes of stress in the workplace

1	Lack of training
2	Relationships at work
3	Excessive workload
4	Poor communication
5	Change and the way change is managed
6	Lack of control over own role
7	Lack of support
8	Lack of clarity on role
9	Unreasonable demands

Ways to help maintain your health and well-being

1	Talking to friends, family and co-workers when you have a problem and seeking practical and emotional support whilst maintaining confidentiality.

2	Eating healthy and avoiding harmful levels of alcohol or other stimulants.

3	Take physical exercise or using meditation to release stress.

4	Resolving any personal conflicts or relationship issues.

5	Take time to relax and do things you enjoy.

6	Try to understand your limitations and your job limitations.

7   Learn to say no and overextending yourself.

8   Learn to master your professional craft by being aware of triggers and warning signs of stress both in yourself and your charges to be able to avoid stress.

Reflection

Reflecting on past events is a natural way of coping and understanding them to improve in the future.

It may be useful to ask yourself the following to aid your reflection:

1   Am I overacting?

2   Am I taking this too personally?

3   Could I be misinterpreting the situation?

4   Could I take time out to de-escalate the situation?

5   What other options are available for dealing with the type of situation?

6   Who can I talk to about this?

7   What will make me less stressed over the situation?

8   What additional support I can ask for?

A study carried out by Lancaster University in 2016 revealed that workers in the health and social care are twice as likely to suffer from stress and depression.

Protecting yourself from aggressive behaviour

To insure your well-being when dealing with individuals with challenging behaviour it is important to avoid injury resulting from any aggressive behaviour, therefore you should:

1. Follow your organisation's policies.
2. Clear the space to make it as safe as possible.
3. Remove others from the danger.
4. Speak to the individual in a calm, clear and non-provocative way.
5. Give the individual enough space.
6. Maintain a safe distance.
7. Use a calm tone of voice to calm them.
8. Use diversion techniques if possible, try to distract them by giving them something else to think about or do.
9. Contact other members of staff as soon as possible for support.
10. If necessary contact emergency support teams internally, such as the mental health team, or even emergency services (police, ambulance).

Support in the workplace

Within your organisation. you can use the following support systems if they are available.

1. Employee assistance programmes.
2. Occupational health support.
3. Independent counsellors.
4. Confidential phone-line support.
5. A sympathetic ear for all staff, for example a buddy system.
6. Specialist support for example such as a mental health team or a psychologist.

7	Training to ensure that staff are working within their responsibilities.
8	Regular health checks.
9	Phased return to work policy.
10	Ensuring that certain staff are not involved with the care of certain individuals, maybe through changing of hours or staff.
11	Provision of regular meetings with the line manger to keep an individual with challenging behaviour's care-plan current.
12	Sports and social activities as composed by your organisation.

Staff at most risk

Research by Cairncross and Kitson in 2013, found 55% of social care workers reported verbal abuse and 52% reported physical abuse within a twelve month period.

Staff who are most at risk from injury and abuse from individuals with challenging behaviour.

1	Lone workers
2	Staff that deal with individuals with learning disabilities.
3	Staff that deal with individuals with dementia.
4	Staff that deal with individuals with mental health issues.
5	Staff that deal with individuals with substance abuse issues.

Answer to question 22: Describe the importance of accessing appropriate support systems:

In is important to maintain your good health especially under stressful conditions to keep the quality of your care high and constant. **A healthy workforce benefits the organisation,** garnering a more positive, safe and healthy environment. An increase in morale and less absenteeism which leads to **reduced costs for the organisation.**

For you as a professional carer accessing the right support will reduce your work related stress and reduce work related health problems.

Effects of work related stressed

Work related stress can effect you physically, mentally and your own behaviour.

Physical effects

1. Sleep disturbance
2. Stomach problems
3. Tiredness
4. Chest pains
5. Palpitations
6. High blood pressure
7. Headaches
8. Muscle pain

Mental effects

1. Sadness
2. Depression
3. Anxiety
4. Irritability
5. Mood swings
6. Restlessness
7. Lack of motivation
8. Reduced concentration
9. Feeling overwhelmed

Behavioural effects

1. Drug or alcohol dependency
2. Increased tobacco use.
3. Appetite problems.
4. Bouts of anger.

5   Increased frustration/aggression.
6   Becoming socially isolated.
7   Lack of motivation.

Staying well allows you to perform well and increase the success of your care. Seeking the right support helps you stay well, and avoid risk and long-term health problems related to work.

Thank you very much in taking the time to review my work.

Pedro Ramalho

Printed in Great Britain
by Amazon